mrac

This is a
× × × × ×
PERSONAL
DIARY

Written
&
Conjured
× by ×

Spooky (Me!)

It's my True (mostly) life story!

Carine-M

Élian Black'mor

Spooky

& THE STRANGE

TALES

VOLUME 1

MONSTER

Inn

EDITOR'S NOTE

SPOOKY'S DIARY IS QUITE UNIQUE. IT ORIGINALLY HOPED TO BE A BOOK OF FAIRY TALES, BUT WITH THAT DREAM UNREALIZED IT WAS REPURPOSED — BY A LOVING FAIRY GODMOTHER — INTO THE PERSONAL DIARY OF A SPECIAL LITTLE GIRL.

★

MUCH TO THE BOOK'S DISAPPOINTMENT, IT IS NOT AS LARGE OR IMPRESSIVE AS IT MAY HAVE BEEN, HAD IT BEEN A REAL BOOK OF FAIRY TALES. BUT LUCKILY FOR SPOOKY, IT HAS THE MOST IMPORTANT CHARACTERISTICS OF ALL THE BEST FAIRY TALE BOOKS... INSPIRED BY THE VIVID EXPERIENCES OF ITS OWNER AND ABLE TO ILLUSTRATE HER STORIES SPOOKILY!

IT IS THE PERFECT YOUNG GIRL'S COMPANION. AND SINCE IT ONLY OPENS FOR ITS RIGHTFUL OWNER, IT NEEDS NO LOCK OR KEY. BUT BEWARE: ONCE OPENED, IT WON'T SHUT UP!

SO DON'T BE SURPRISED IF YOU SEE THIS ICON 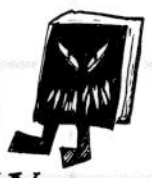
IT JUST MEANS THE BOOK HAD TO HAVE ITS SAY...

Prologue
Departure from Fairytale Land

To where the 3 WEE PIGGIES ARE GOING TO Rule THE Roost

HIGGEDY PIGGEDY

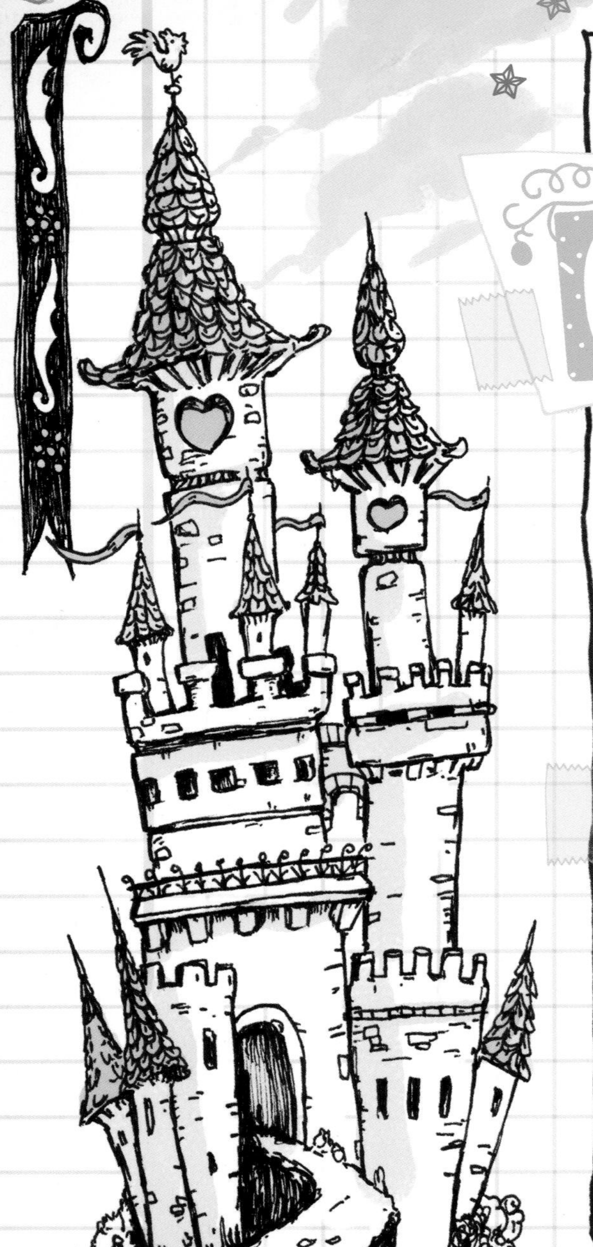

Once upon a time, in the heart of Fairytale Land, there was a king and queen who had the strangest child.

Her skin was as white as milk
and her hair was as black as silk...

...Bla, bla, blee...that princess is me...
...and let me tell you about who I came to be...

When I was born, my godmother blessed me with the greatest things ever: the gift of gab and a very wild imagination.

(Well that's what my parents say about me anyway!)

And with a magic thinking spell,
HIGGEDY PIGGEDY everything I wish for,
comes out quite well.

(and I think that's just fantastic!!)

Especially when I run into frogs.

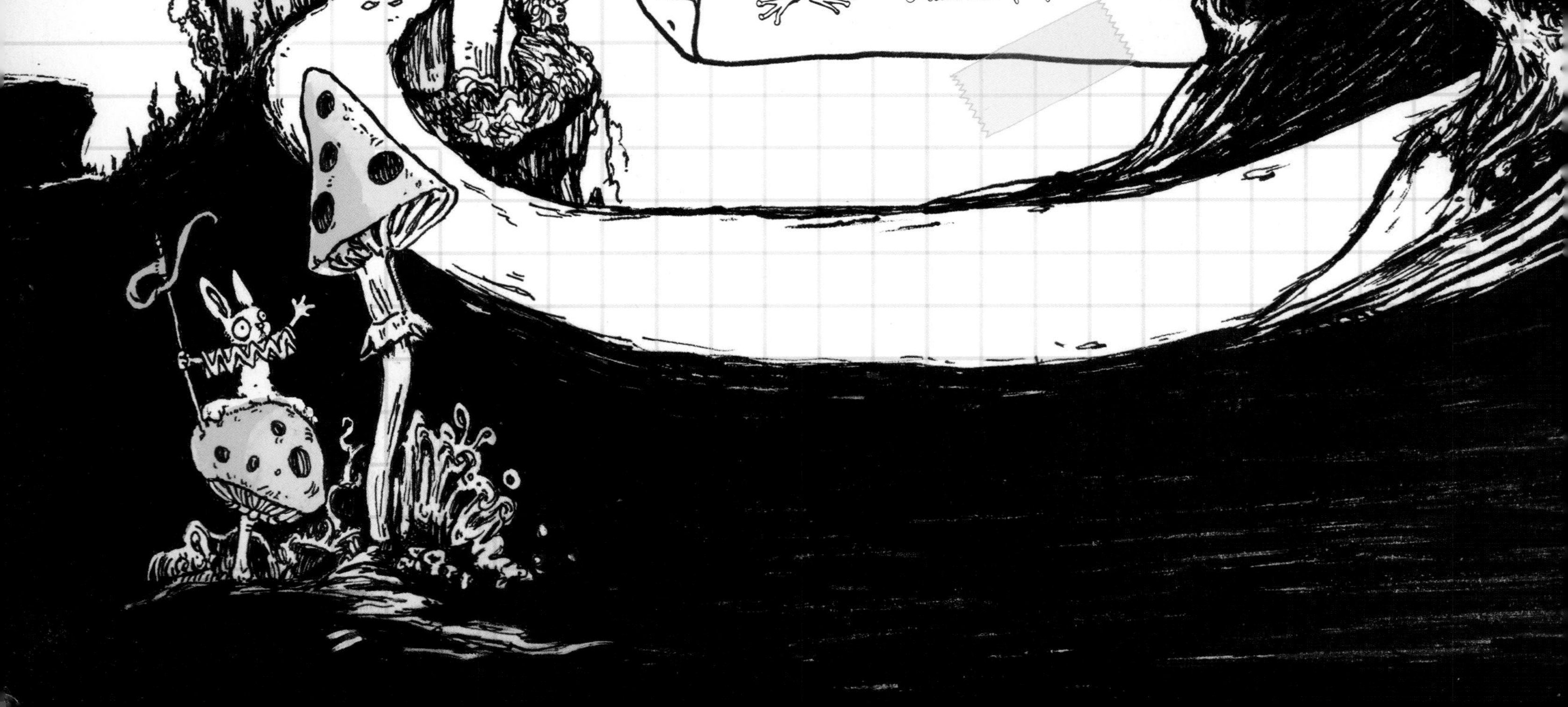

POOF! PING!

Whenever I go out
to have a bit of fun,
with a HIGGEDY PIGGEDY Poof! Ping!
It's disasters by the ton!
(hee, hee, hee!)

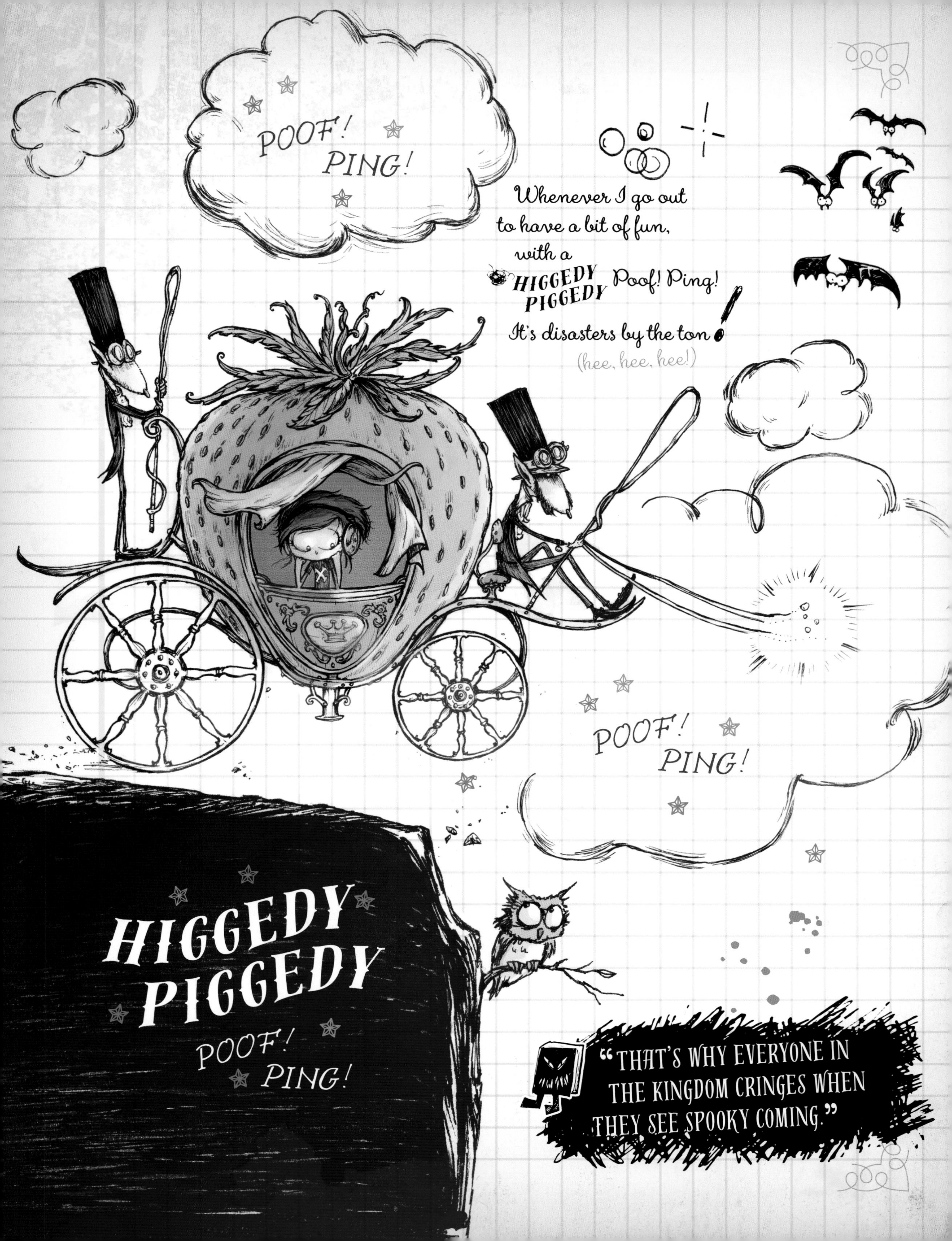
POOF! PING!

HIGGEDY PIGGEDY
POOF! PING!

"THAT'S WHY EVERYONE IN THE KINGDOM CRINGES WHEN THEY SEE SPOOKY COMING."

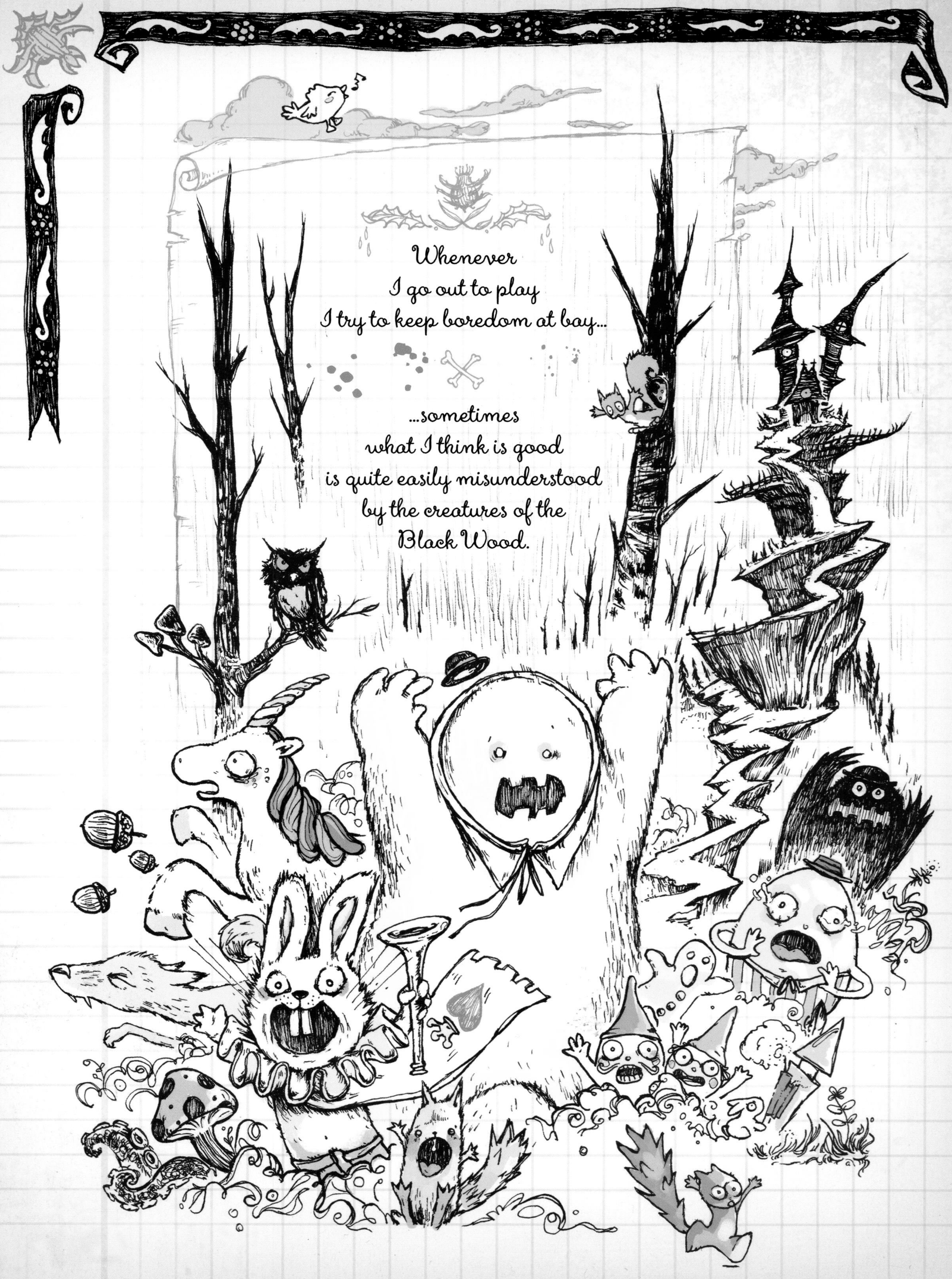

Whenever
I go out to play
I try to keep boredom at bay...

...sometimes
what I think is good
is quite easily misunderstood
by the creatures of the
Black Wood.

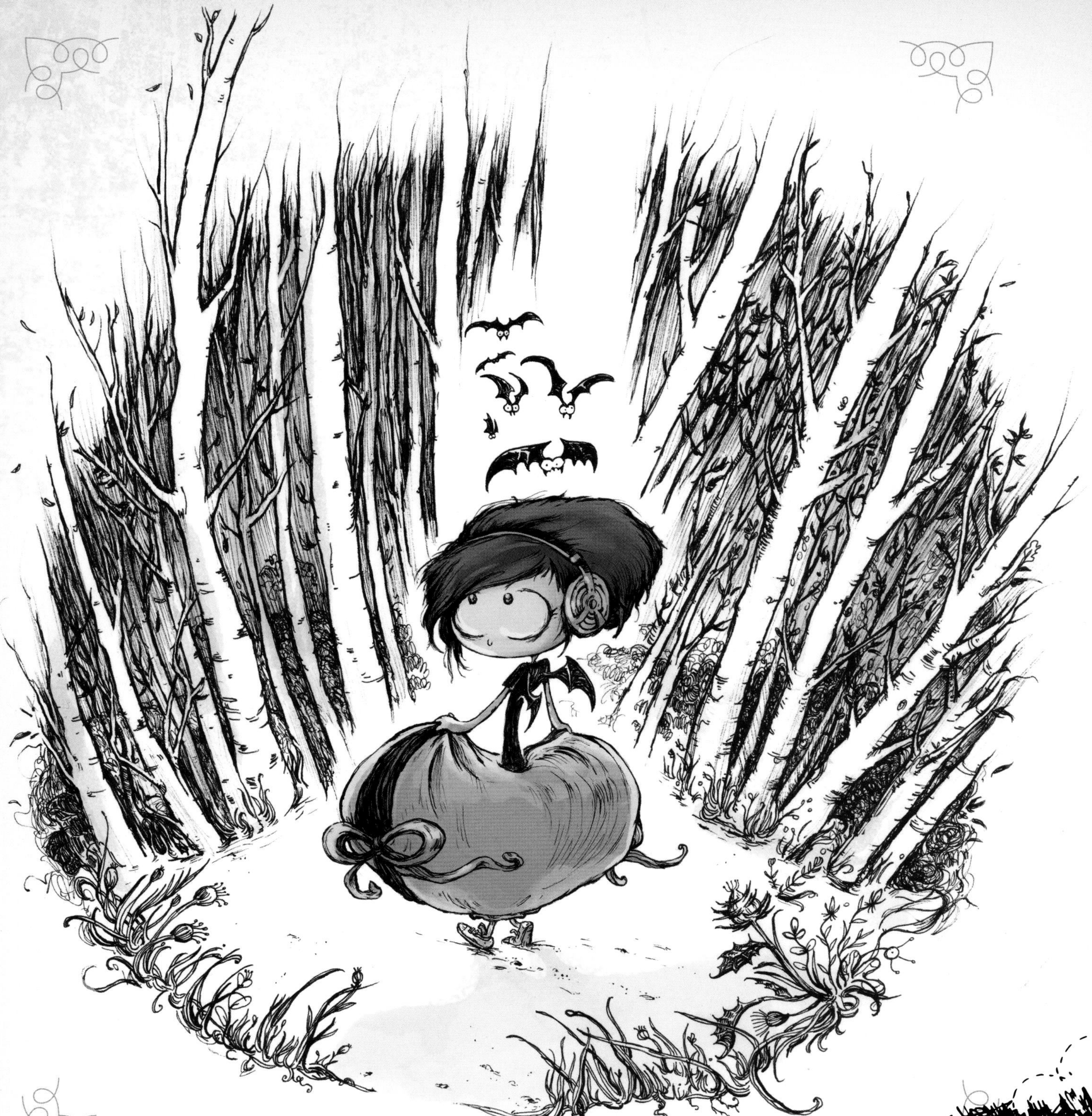

Black Wood

My wanderings can lead to funny, frightening ends...
And drive my parents round the bend.

"EVER SINCE 'ENOUGH'S ENOUGH!' HAS BECOME 'SPOOK'S TOO MUCH!'"

Like all princesses
I have a magic mirror.
(That often lies and teases.)

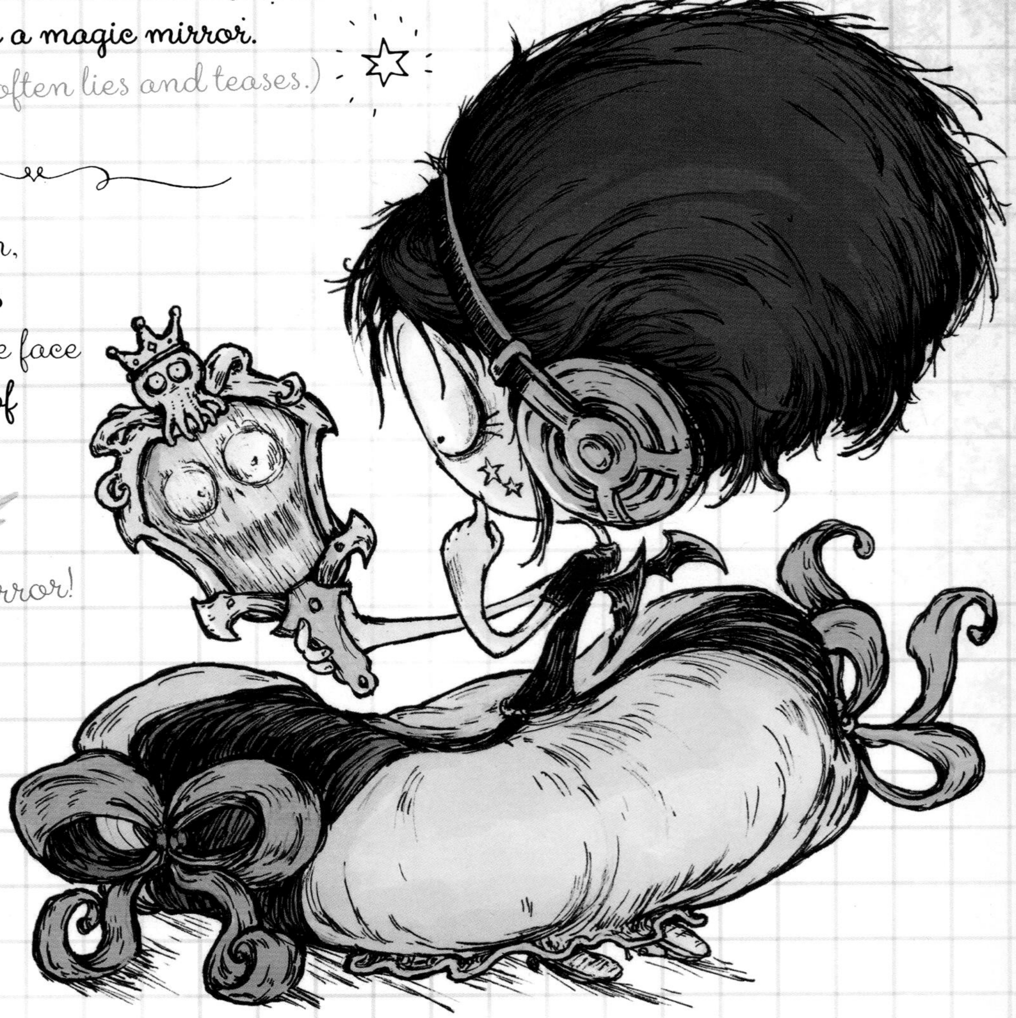

Of my reflection,
I see **only traces**
it's mostly a pale face
with odd **tales of
strange places.**

Mirror! Mirror!

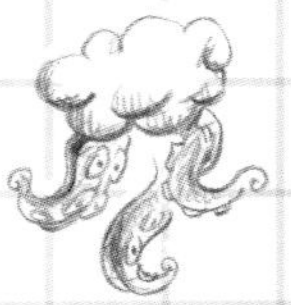

My name's **Spooky**,
I'm from Fairytale Land
and I love to make up
scary stories

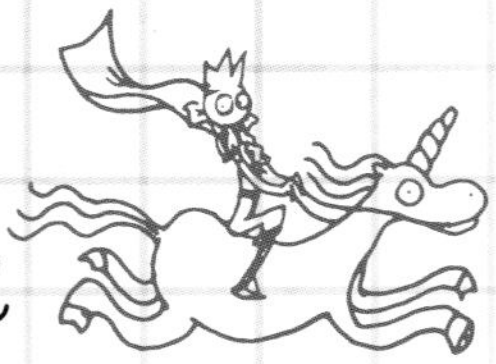

with the help of
my personal diary.

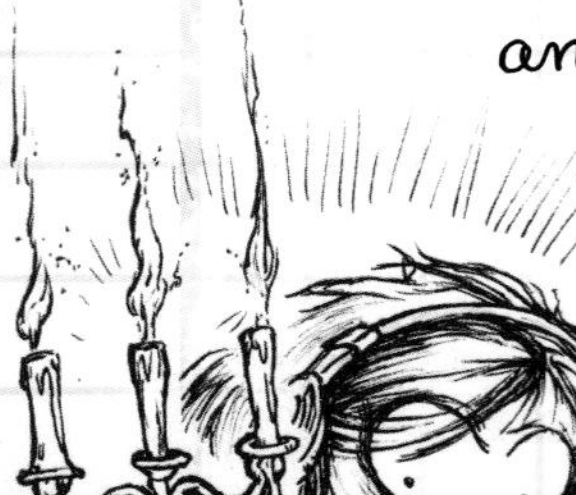

And that's what really
bugs my parents.

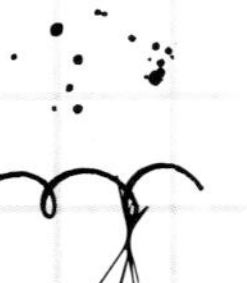

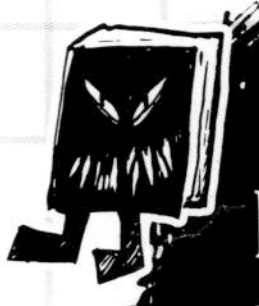

"AND WHAT BUGS ME,
IS THAT I'M NOT
REALLY SUPPOSED TO BE
A PERSONAL DIARY.
ONE DAY, I'LL BE A BIG THICK
BOOK OF FAIRYTALES."

(Yes, one that tells
my life story!)

 Mirror, mirror!

 My *My* Magic mirror

Mirror, mirror, please reveal! (Twice*)
What dark, dark corners can conceal!

*Repeat this chant
not once, but thrice,
then touch the mirror,
and be concise.
(I haven't had an answer yet...)

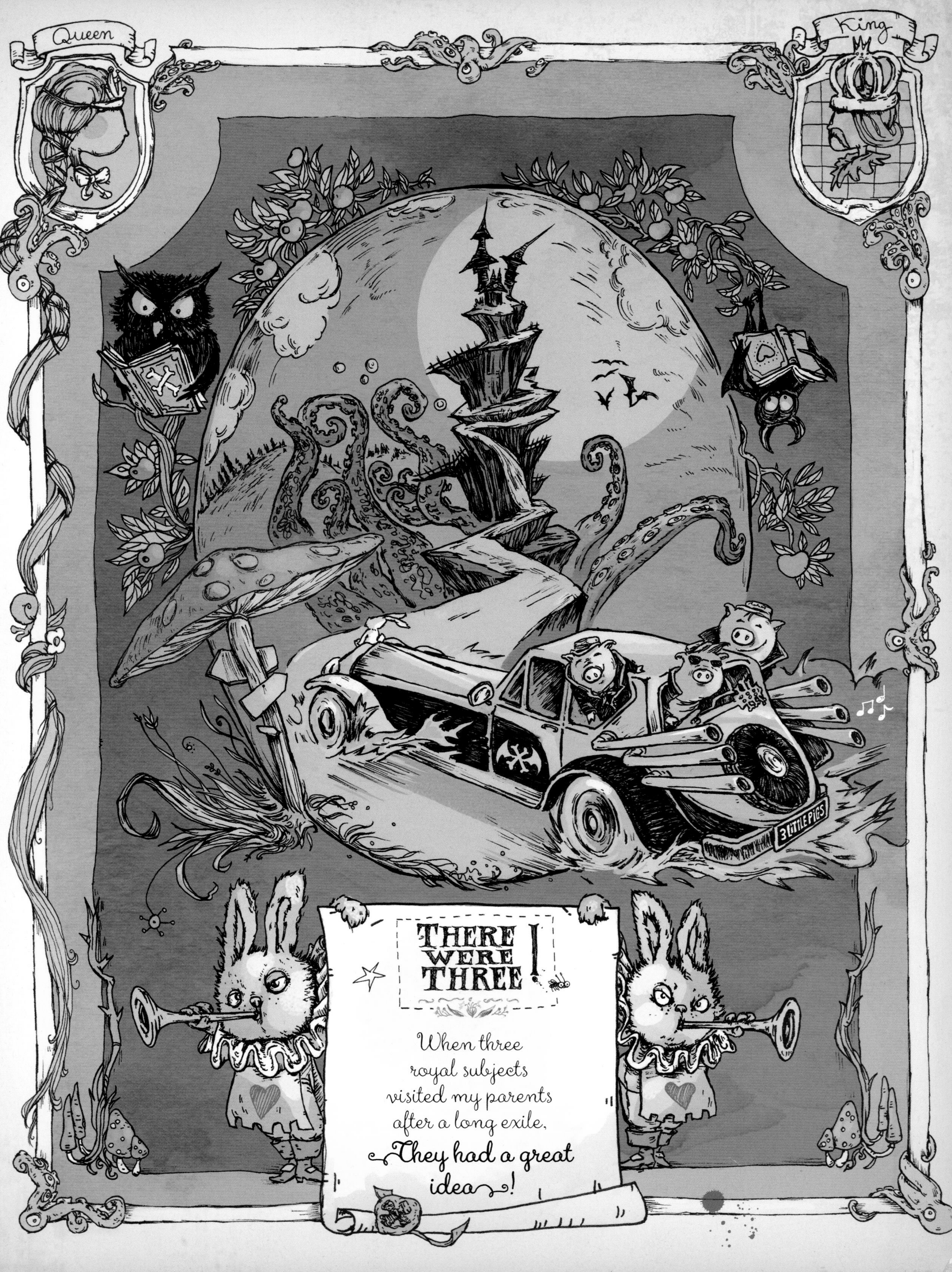
Queen
King
3 LITTLE PIGS
THERE WERE THREE !
When three royal subjects visited my parents after a long exile,
They had a great idea!

Tiger

They're amazing!
They're charming, talented
and they've been nearly
everywhere in the whole world.

Marshal

Stan

THE FAMOUS
✳ Popular ✳
3 LITTLE PIGS ❤
100% ORIGINAL
Rock Stars

My uncles, the famous Three Little Pigs, are big celebrities in our kingdom... highly respected for their ingenuity.
(Especially since the Big Bad Wolf thing.)

So, when Tiger (the smart one), offered to take me with them to their new gothic inn they just bought on Gray's Inn Road in the heart of London... ...my parents (you guessed it) were thrilled.

DEVIL!

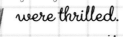

I knew they were coming as soon as I heard Von Drats' "Phantom Chop" playing, off in the distance.

In exchange for 3 mushrooms.

Before I left

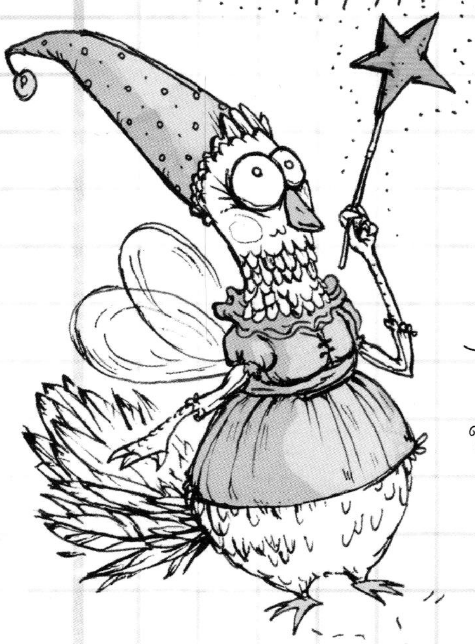

My godmother insisted on giving me 3 presents:

An awesome pen

While writing in black,
sometimes it makes **spots in blue!**
(and tons of other colors too...)
Very Cool!

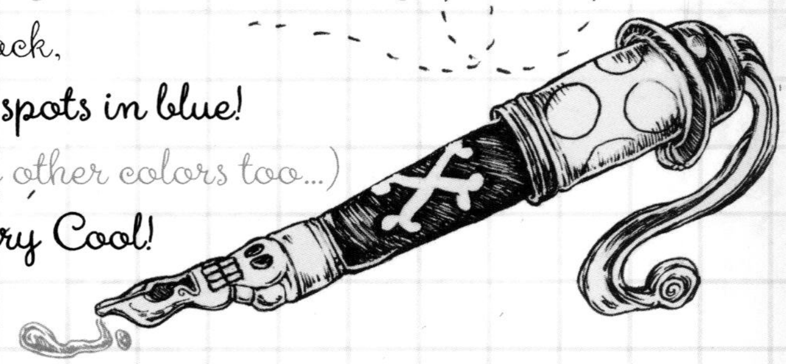

A (much improved) book of tales

It failed as a book of fairytales
So my big-hearted godmother turned it into
a special personal diary for me!
Which I am using to tell my story.
(Its comments aren't always nice,
But that's okay, it'll suffice.)

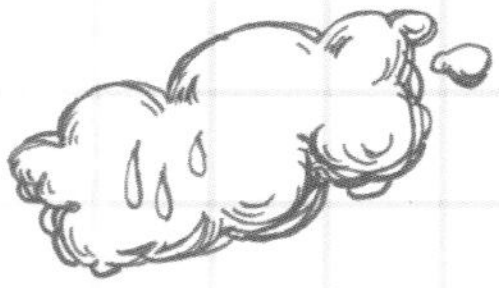

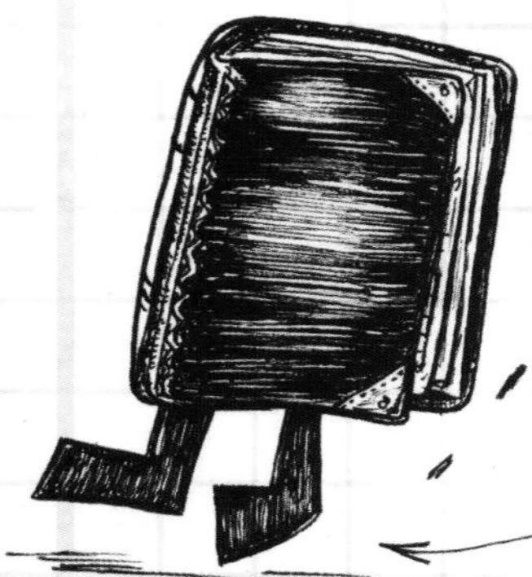

It likes to wear eccentric shoes,
especially the ones knights use!

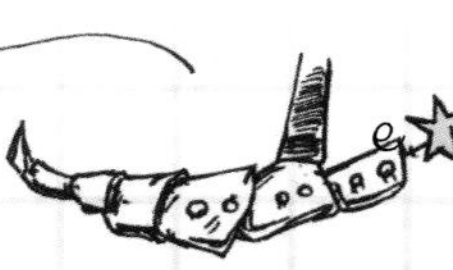

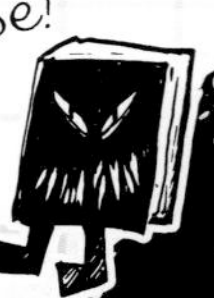

"THEY'RE MUCH MORE COMFORTABLE THAN SNEAKERS."

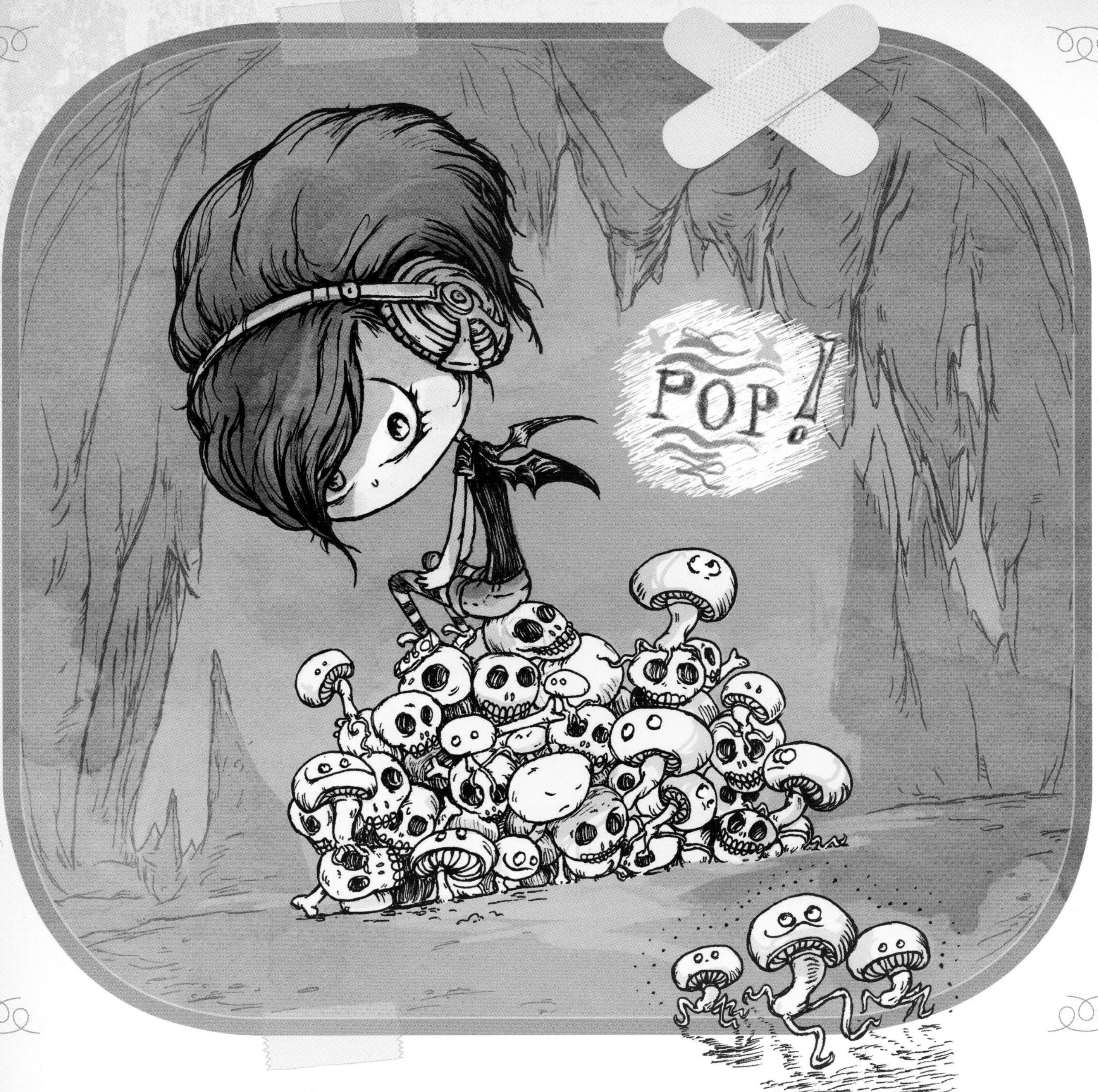
POP!

And a tee-shirt with wings in back.

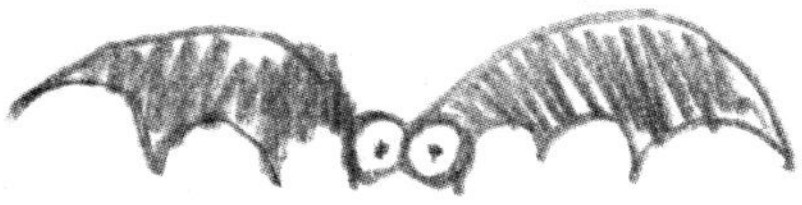

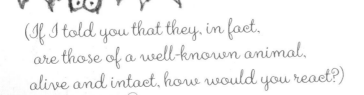

(If I told you that they, in fact,
are those of a well-known animal,
alive and intact, how would you react?)

(All of that
in exchange
for **3 catacomb mushrooms.**
I should mention that
catacomb mushrooms
are definitely not easy
to catch!)

Once Upon a Time

My departure

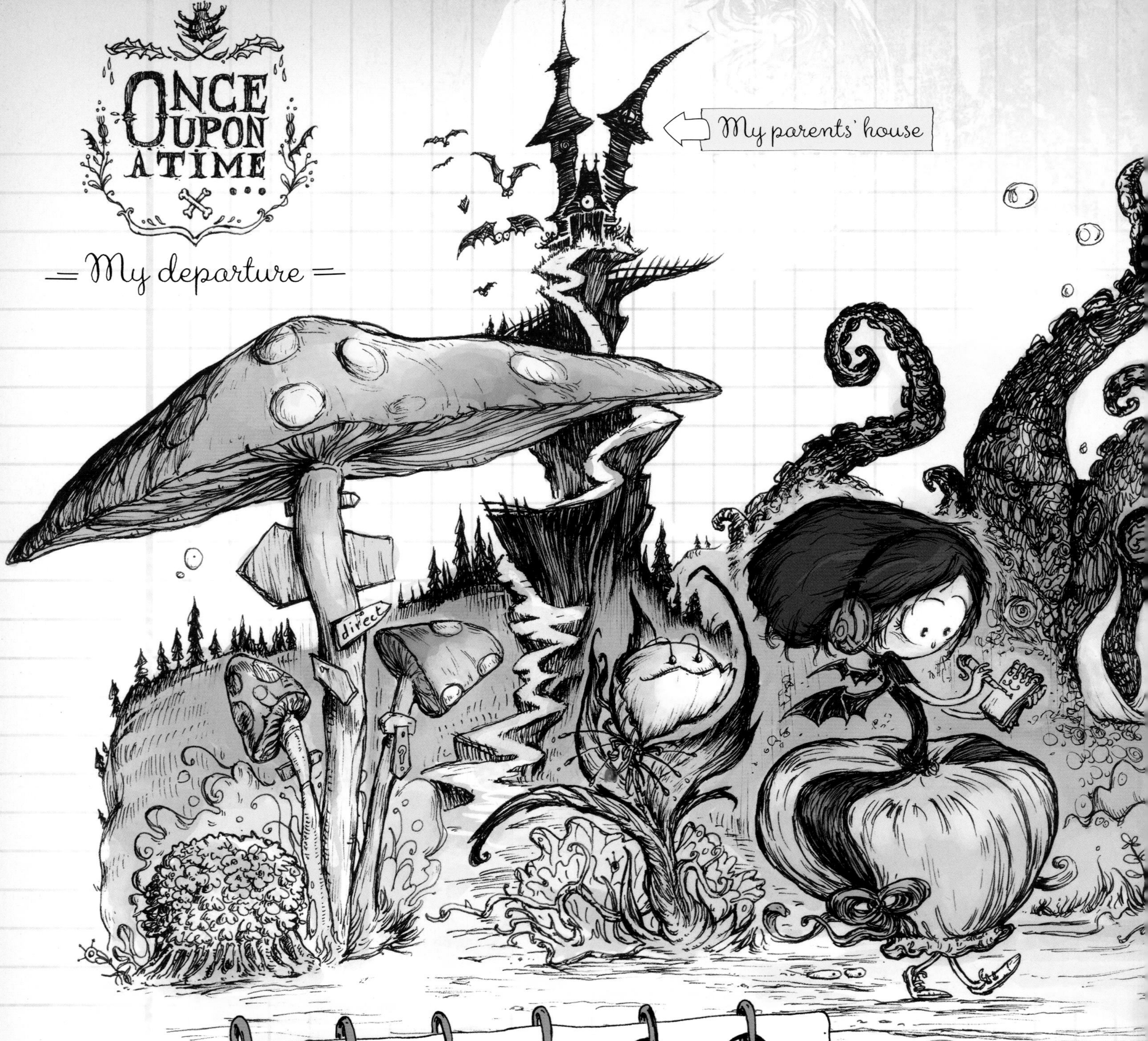
My parents' house
direct

List of things to absolutely not forget:

× × ×

Marshy Eucomis Gigas seeds – since it is traditional to take them with you when you leave Fairytale Land.

4 pounds of Monster tea with bergamot.

And most importantly, my special tornado umbrella.

This is the portal! Do I need to specify that it is one of those special places that are "**bigger on the inside**"?

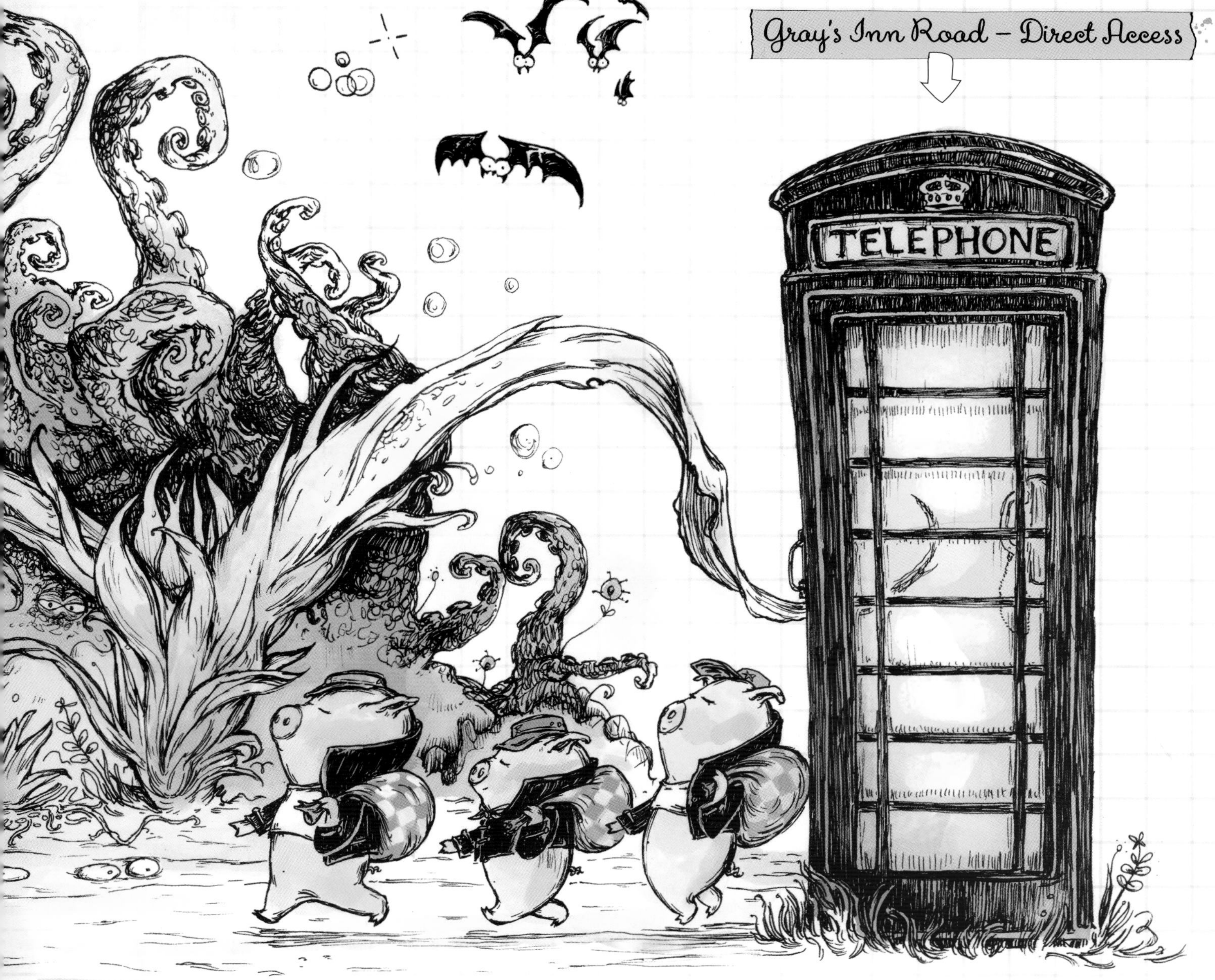
Gray's Inn Road – Direct Access
TELEPHONE

As my parents started to hesitate, **my 3 uncles were very quick to take my luggage to the inn on Gray's Inn Road.**

(They're the best!)

(...Hmmmmm! I am known for being rather chatty, but I'm not going to say any more right now. **I'll let you discover the rest for yourself...**)

Chapter 1
Mysteries, Monsters and Jam

London
WHERE THE STRANGE
MEETS
THE
Everyday.

NO KEY, NO ENTRY!
NO VACANCY!

amazing!

IT'S *got everything* I LOVE

Incredible!! Before I even arrived my room was filled with all the things I love!! From the Will-o'wisps dancing in the Kraken chimney to the monster on the bed! Everything here is done with heart. I already feel at home. My uncles have great taste. They're taking super care of me and I lovvvvve Mr. Duster. ♡

He's too cool! He's a first class upstairs ghost.

White as a sheet and loves rock and roll.

I can tell we're really going to get along.

(My personal diary loves quotes...

"ONCE UPON A TIME THERE WAS A LITTLE GIRL WHO WAS LOVED BY ALL... ESPECIALLY HER GRANDMOTHER."

Brothers Grimm

...it's probably due to its deep love of fairytales.)

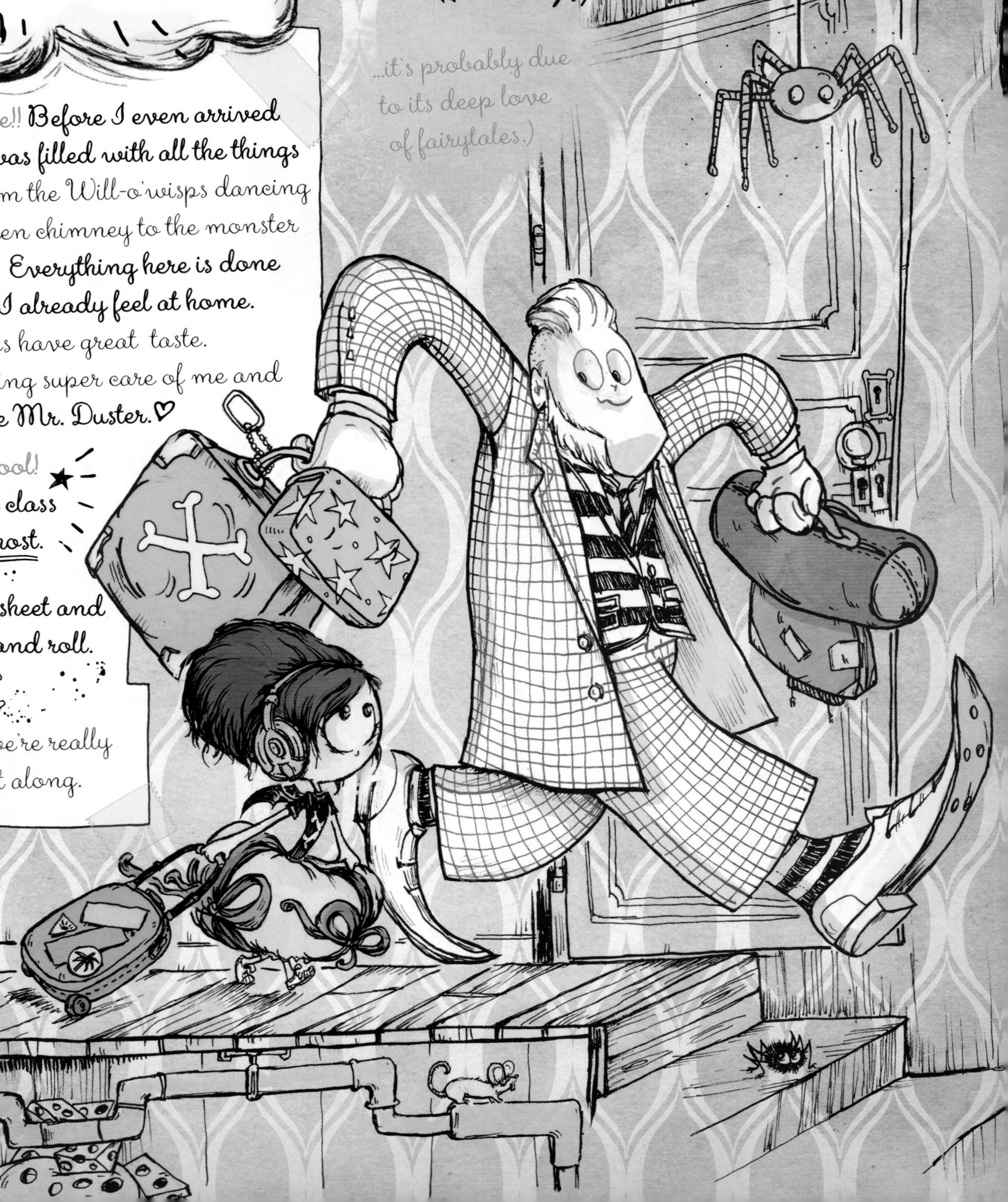

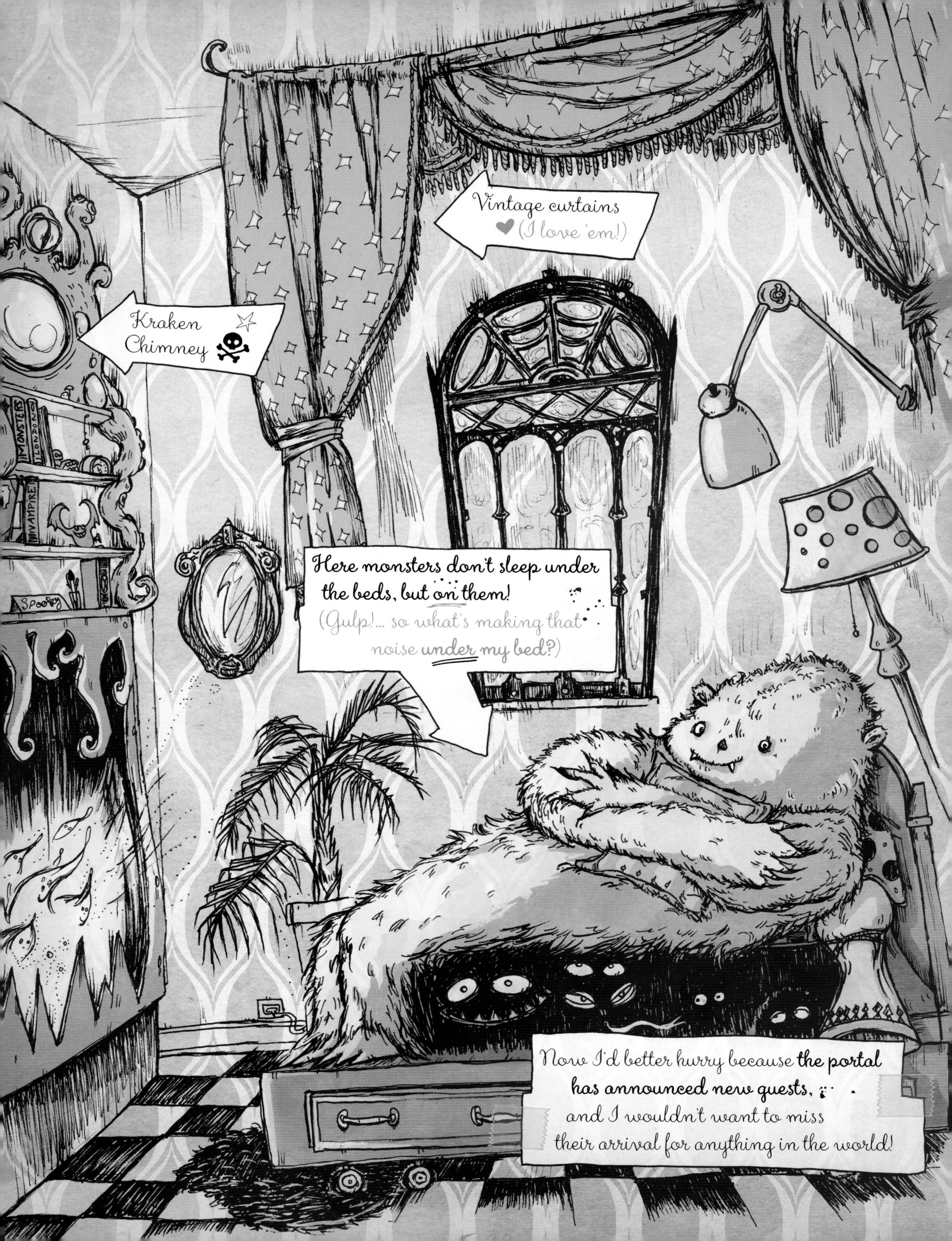
Vintage curtains
(I love 'em!)
Kraken Chimney
Here monsters don't sleep under the beds, but on them!
(Gulp!... so what's making that noise under my bed?)
Now I'd better hurry because the portal has announced new guests,
and I wouldn't want to miss their arrival for anything in the world!

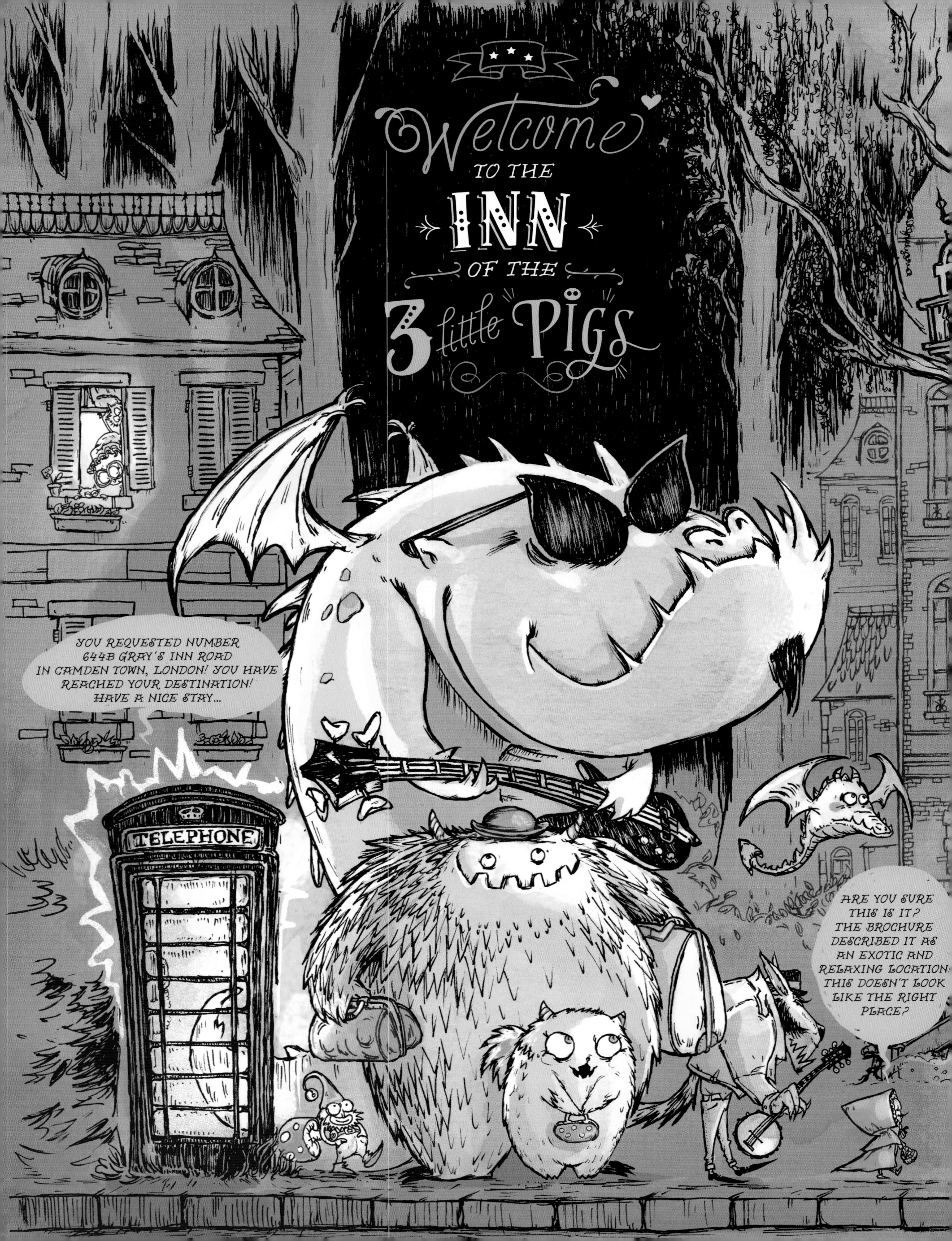
Welcome TO THE INN OF THE 3 little PIGS
YOU REQUESTED NUMBER 644B GRAY'S INN ROAD IN CAMDEN TOWN, LONDON! YOU HAVE REACHED YOUR DESTINATION! HAVE A NICE STAY...
TELEPHONE
ARE YOU SURE THIS IS IT? THE BROCHURE DESCRIBED IT AS AN EXOTIC AND RELAXING LOCATION. THIS DOESN'T LOOK LIKE THE RIGHT PLACE?

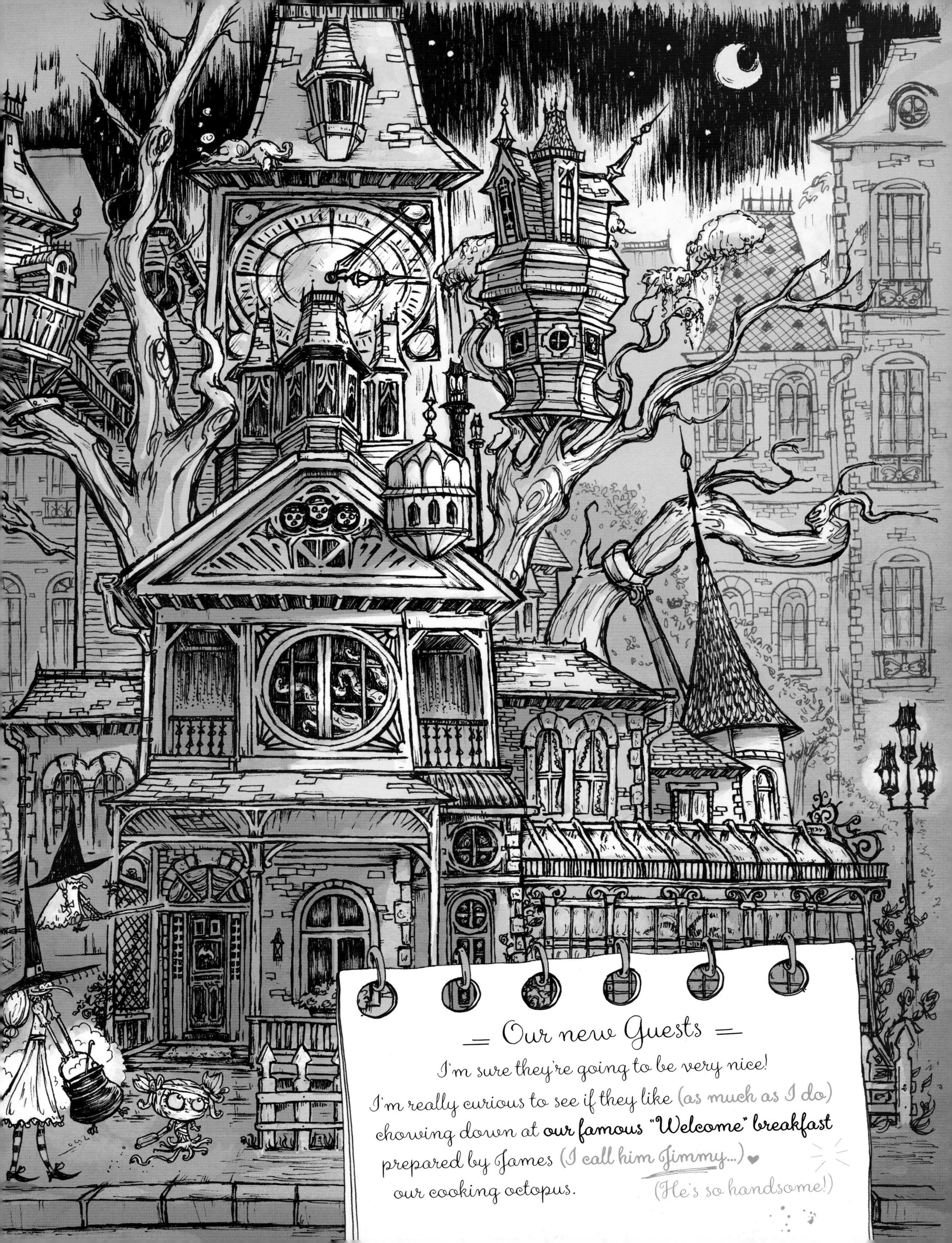
— Our new Guests —
I'm sure they're going to be very nice!
I'm really curious to see if they like (as much as I do)
chowing down at **our famous "Welcome" breakfast**
prepared by James (I call him Jimmy...) ♥
our cooking octopus.
(He's so handsome!)

And POOF no more JAM

The new guests started arriving and everyone was aflutter! We didn't know if we were coming or going! Between showing them their rooms, explaining the rules in all the different languages the guests spoke, and everyone wanting something to eat straight away, we were completely overwhelmed. Luckily, Jimmy — not just handsome but clever, too — had baked some of his famous Choco-chompo welcome muffins. Otherwise, I'm sure some of the guests would have chomped down on us!

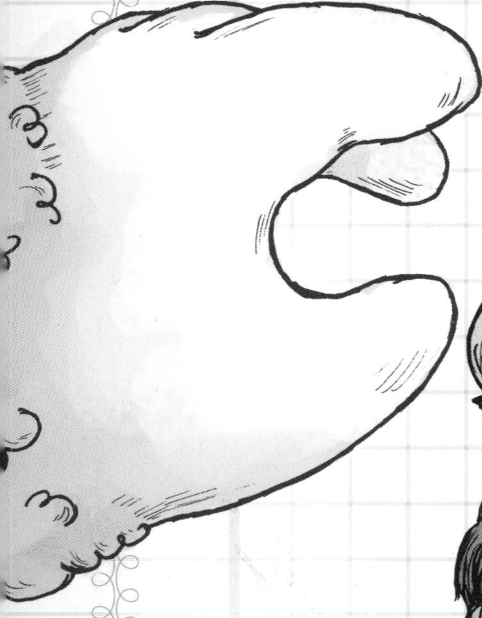

Once all the guests were settled in and the chomping was averted, we all gathered in the breakfast room.

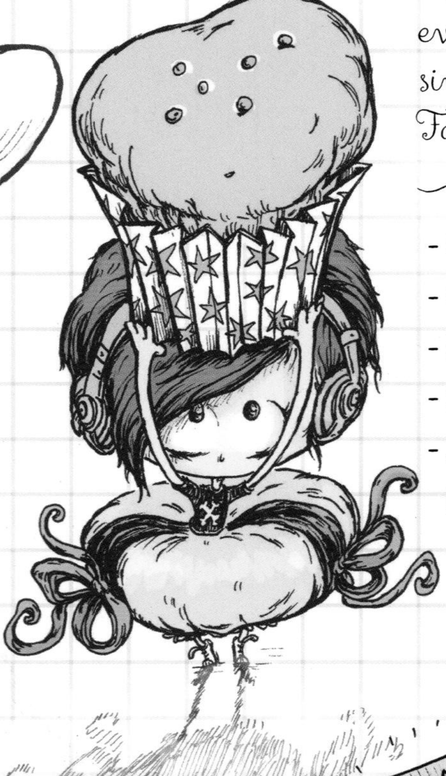

Everyone seemed to be there, well... I think everyone was there, but it's hard to tell, especially since visitors aren't chaperoned like we are in Fairytale Land.

The menu's really yummy, don't you think?

- **Choco-chompos, Bergamot tea**
- **Eggs and (perfectly cooked) bacon**
- **Papaya — fresh from Hawaii**
- **Danish and Giant Croissants (for the French guests!)**
- **And, of course, our famous home baked sliced bread (toasted). It's unionized!**

(The loaves always go on strike when **they're spread with jam** — it's soo funny.)

But that morning (unlike the day I arrived, when jam was plentiful and the toast was on strike) **they were over the moon** (so to speak)...

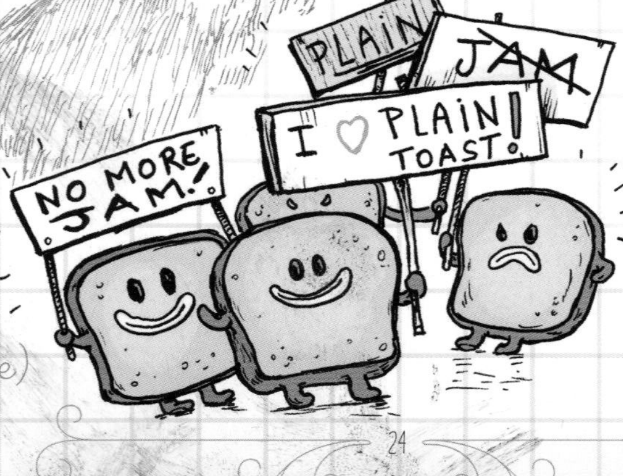
PLAIN
JAM
I ♡ PLAIN TOAST!
NO MORE JAM!

...since all the jam was gone! **We were in a panic, but the slices were thrilled.**

What?! No Jam!
Mister Nightmare looks really disappointed.

Mister
Nightmare

What a crazy way to start my very first day.
Fortunately, my uncles had already contacted their "private investigators."
Security is taken very seriously here... certainly when it comes to breakfast.

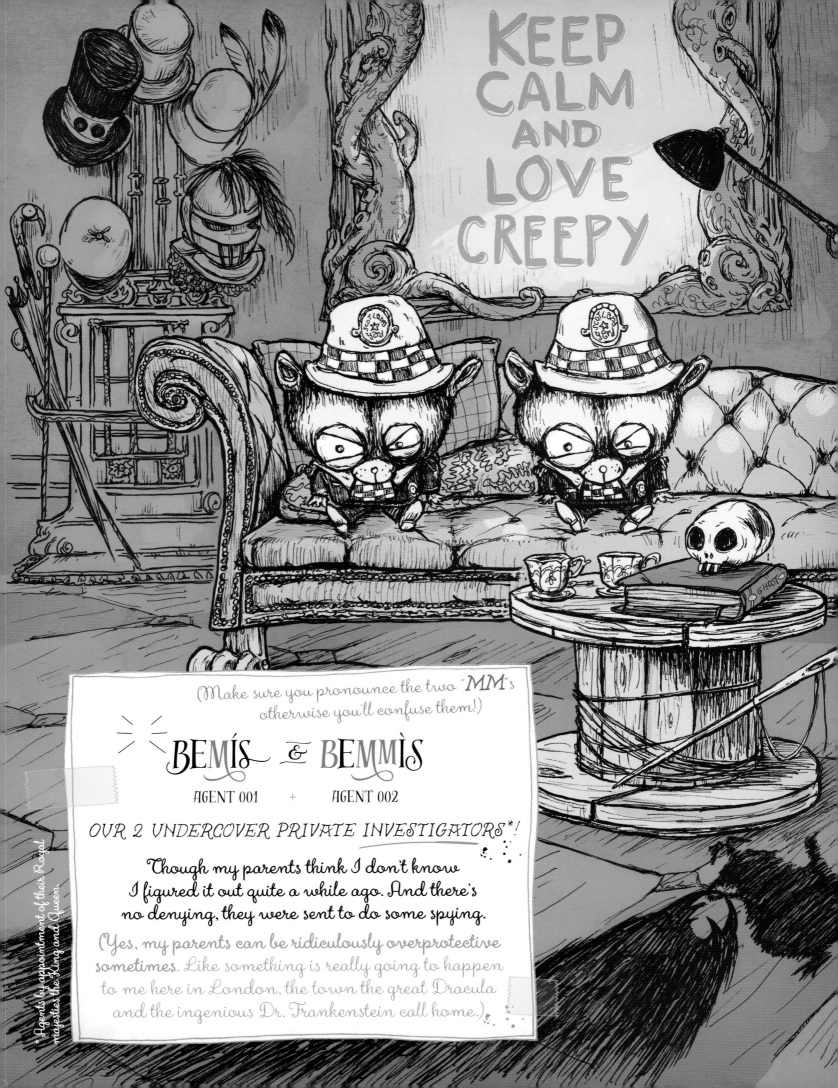

KEEP
CALM
AND
LOVE
CREEPY

(Make sure you pronounce the two "MM"s
otherwise you'll confuse them!)

BEMÍS & BEMMÌS

AGENT 001 + AGENT 002

OVR 2 UNDERCOVER PRIVATE INVESTIGATORS*!

Though my parents think I don't know
I figured it out quite a while ago. And there's
no denying, they were sent to do some spying.

(Yes, my parents can be ridiculously overprotective
sometimes. Like something is really going to happen
to me here in London, the town the great Dracula
and the ingenious Dr. Frankenstein call home.)

* Agents by appointment of their Royal majesties the King and Queen.

I know these PIs, (They're often off base) I'm dying to know if they'll solve this case.

As soon as they arrived, I was listening in...

"(NPN) No panic necessary!" Bemis said. "We're already on the case!" Bemmis added. "We cannot allow this hotel to be victimized by such sabotage, especially considering the extremely V.I.P. V.I.P.s that stay here. Forget the members of the sliced bread union, those guys are way too soft to come up with a scheme like this!" Bemis bragged! (I think it was Bemis. They're so much alike!) "But an ogre after a long trip..." (referring to Mr. Franklin) — "since we all know about the appetites of ogres..." — "He would be ready to do just about anything to impress his pretty ogrette!" (That's Mrs. Franklin)

"Look! Didn't you notice! Since arriving he's always worn something the color of red berry jam..." — "...He's the perfect suspect, don't you think Bemmis?!" — "Absolutely, Bemis! Listen up mister sneaky, don't bother calling your lawyer." — "You're under arrest!!" they said to poor Mister Franklin in unison. But as my Uncle Marshal pointed out (he's the tough one), that didn't make any sense, because from the moment Mr. and Mrs. Franklin arrived they had not been out of his sight! He even remembered their polite refusal of "Choco-chompos."

"No thank you, we'll wait till dinner."

(The whole "appetite of an ogre" theory is an old wives' tale, no need to be a genius to figure that out... "the red berry color" thing on the other hand...?!)

THANK YOU FOR CALLING THE "RETURN TO FAIRYTALE LAND FAST" HELP LINE, PLEASE HOLD.

SIRI

NOT GUILTY

YUM YUM, a cat SMACKS × HIS LIPS ×

KNOCK! KNOCK! KNOOOOCK!

~3 days later while the investigation into the muddy mystery of the inn's missing jam was getting nowhere... There was a banging at the door.

My uncles asked me to go see who was thumping so insistently. I opened the door very carefully, leery of what was on the other side. No way! Can't be! An old granny neighbor jumped at me, screaming like a banshee.

"Milly and I say come and see, come and see what you've done to my poor Chester!" Uh... who, "you?" "I haven't done anything!" I said as we set off next door

(Milly)

(On the way, we bumped into — literally — Miss Red who rushed right by us. Were those jars clinking in her basket?)

THERE WERE ENOUGH FOR ONE EACH IN THE END, EVEN THOUGH I DROPPED ONE.

MADE A MESS.

~ She doesn't live far. In two hops and three skips we were both at her front door. It was wide open and inside... Oh, boy. Inside....
As soon as I saw the place I understood who she was. It was obvious.
My uncles lived in a kind of exotic part of town where the headquarters of the **Old Granny Ghost Hunters Club** was based. A club whose membership was made up principally of old ladies who love a good wild ghost chase. ☠ (boo!)
~ It all came back to me! **This bubbly old granny was Miss Grekinn, president** of that funny old granny club and she loves cats ○○○

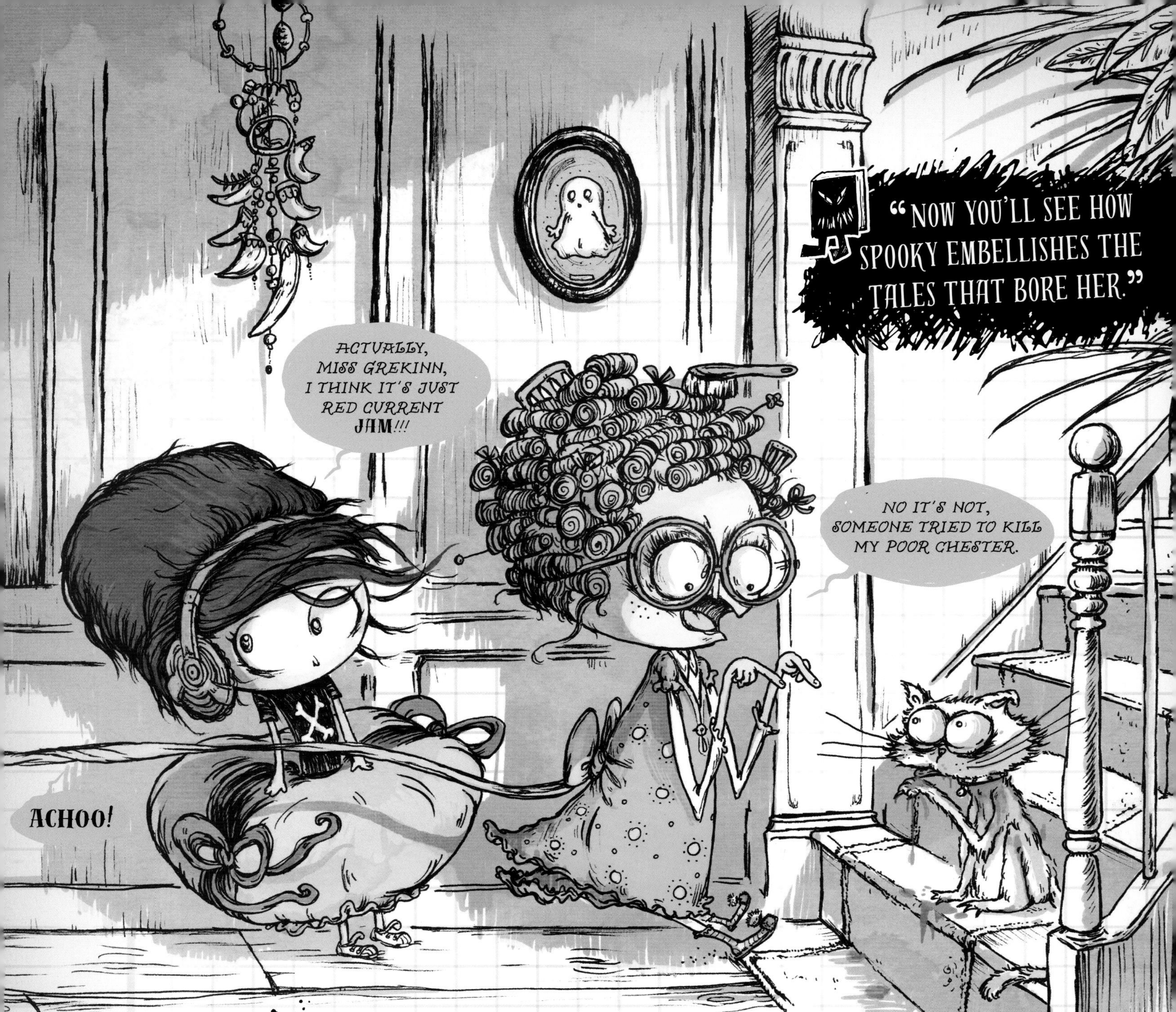
"NOW YOU'LL SEE HOW SPOOKY EMBELLISHES THE TALES THAT BORE HER."
ACTUALLY, MISS GREKINN, I THINK IT'S JUST RED CURRENT JAM!!!
NO IT'S NOT, SOMEONE TRIED TO KILL MY POOR CHESTER.
ACHOO!

Cats! Cats everywhere! Achooooo!! Is what my kitty allergy made me do. Kapoouf!! Is what my godmother's gift made me do! And voila, an instant cat blow dry and shampoo! But Granny Grekinn didn't seem to mind. So, for once, my curse resolved a problem instead of leaving disaster behind. My parents would be proud.

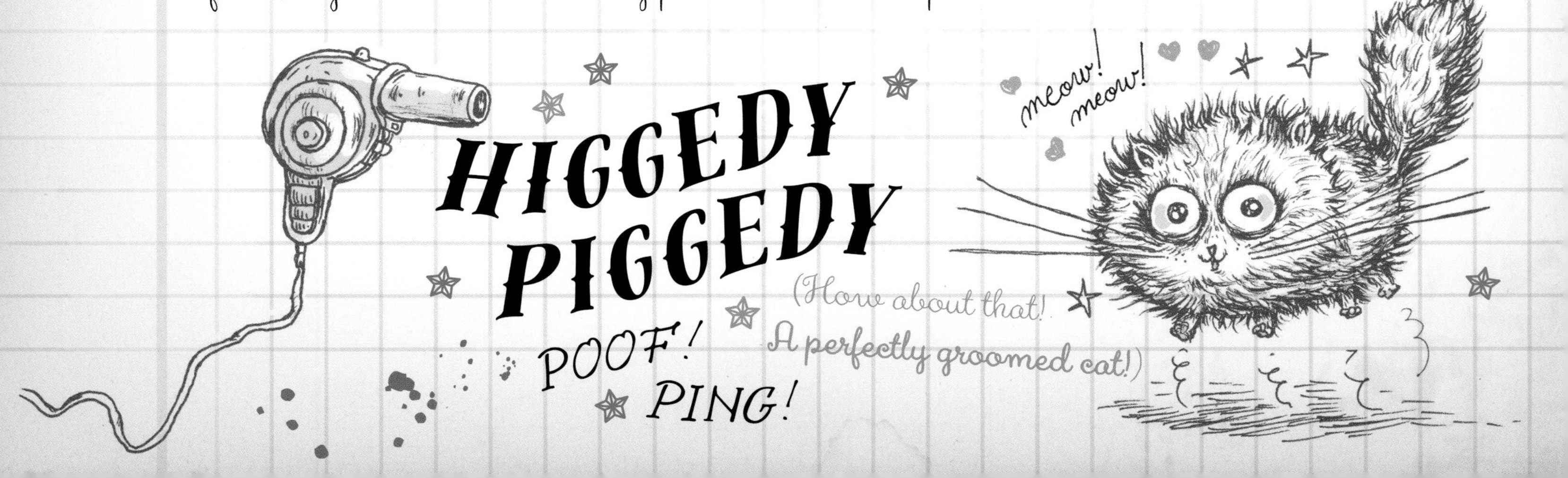
HIGGEDY PIGGEDY
POOF!
PING!
(How about that! A perfectly groomed cat!)
meow! meow!

Little Household and Sarcophagus Intrigues

~I was pretty happy to get back to the inn, away from all that madness, before my luck changed and things turned sour. Speaking of sour, things smelled a bit vinegary, I thought, as I reached the front hall **"white vinegary, in fact!"**

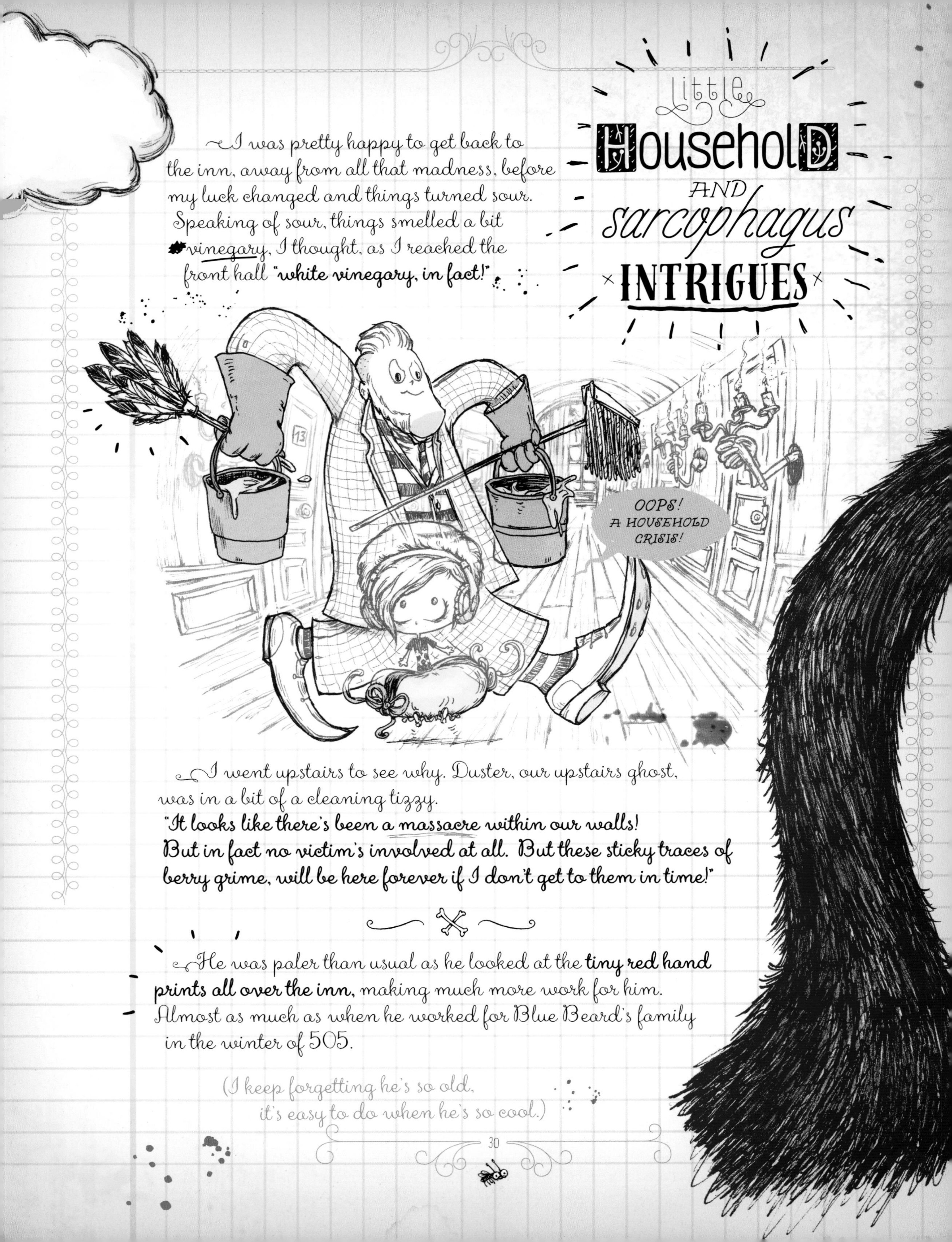
OOPS! A HOUSEHOLD CRISIS!

~I went upstairs to see why. Duster, our upstairs ghost, was in a bit of a cleaning tizzy.
"It looks like there's been a massacre within our walls! But in fact no victim's involved at all. But these sticky traces of berry grime, will be here forever if I don't get to them in time!"

~He was paler than usual as he looked at the **tiny red hand prints all over the inn,** making much more work for him. Almost as much as when he worked for Blue Beard's family in the winter of 505.

(I keep forgetting he's so old, it's easy to do when he's so cool.)

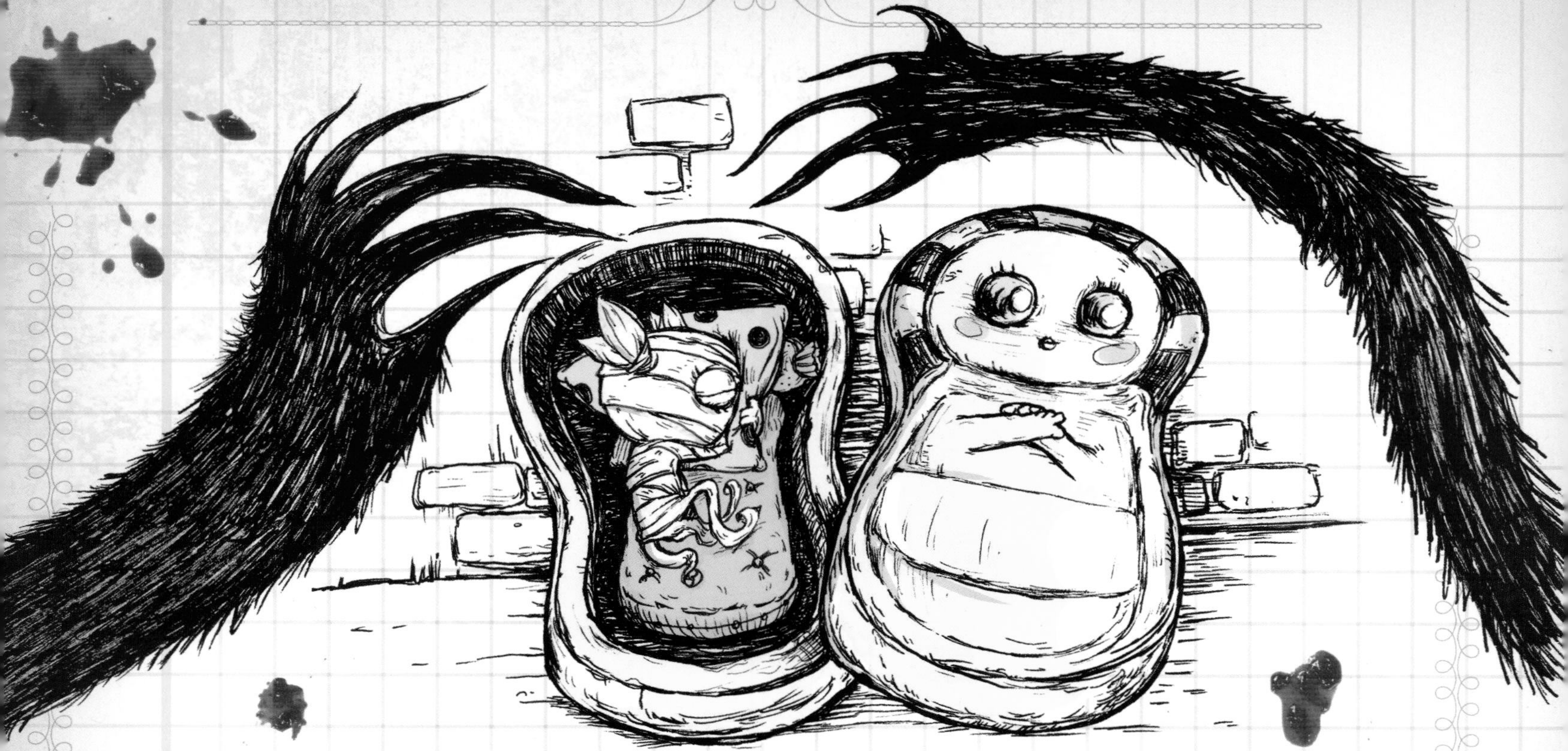

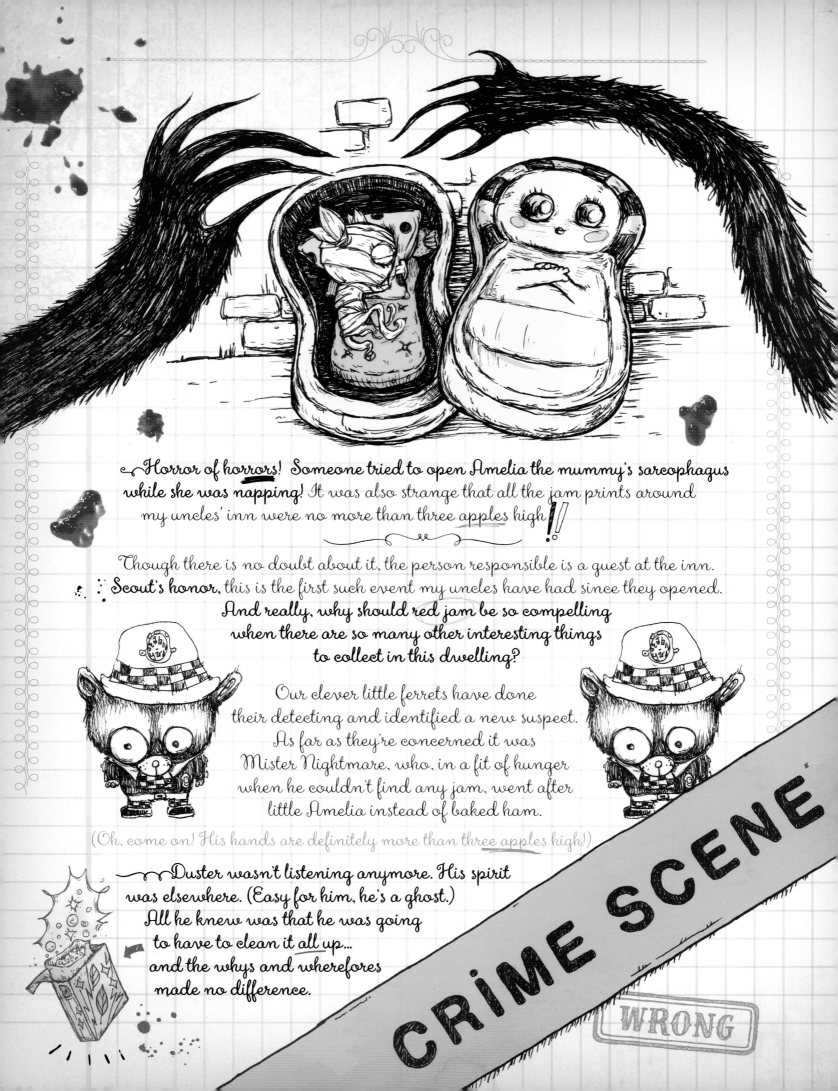

Horror of horrors! Someone tried to open Amelia the mummy's sarcophagus while she was napping! It was also strange that all the jam prints around my uncles' inn were no more than three apples high!!

Though there is no doubt about it, the person responsible is a guest at the inn. Scout's honor, this is the first such event my uncles have had since they opened.

And really, why should red jam be so compelling when there are so many other interesting things to collect in this dwelling?

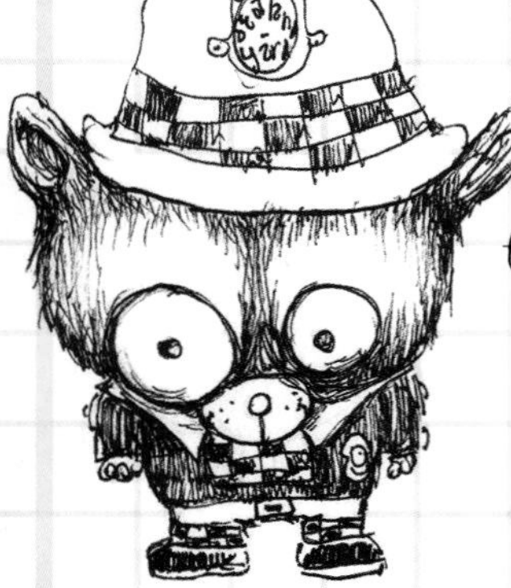

Our clever little ferrets have done their detecting and identified a new suspect. As far as they're concerned it was Mister Nightmare, who, in a fit of hunger when he couldn't find any jam, went after little Amelia instead of baked ham.

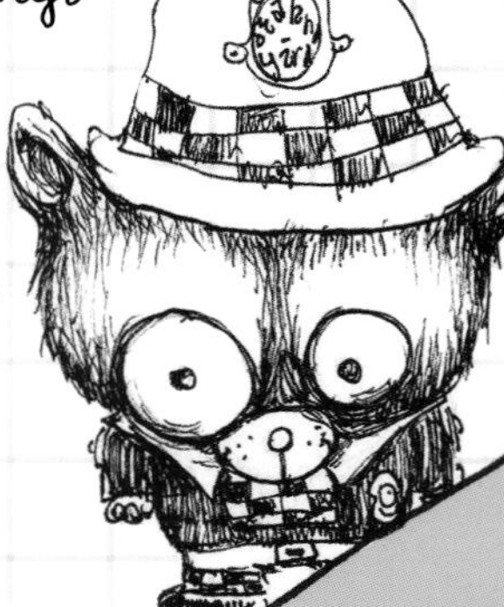

(Oh, come on! His hands are definitely more than three apples high!)

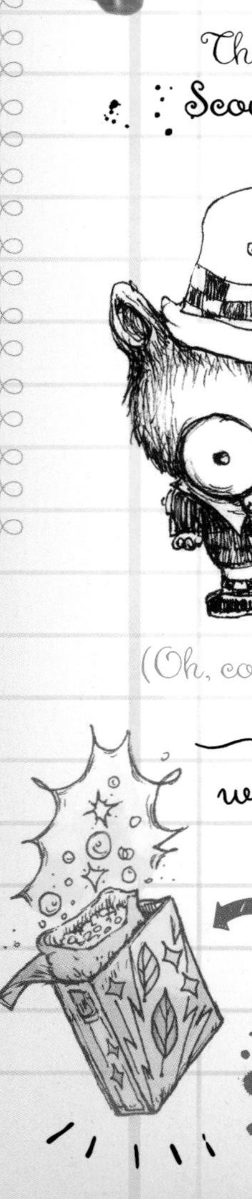

Duster wasn't listening anymore. His spirit was elsewhere. (Easy for him, he's a ghost.) All he knew was that he was going to have to clean it all up... and the whys and wherefores made no difference.

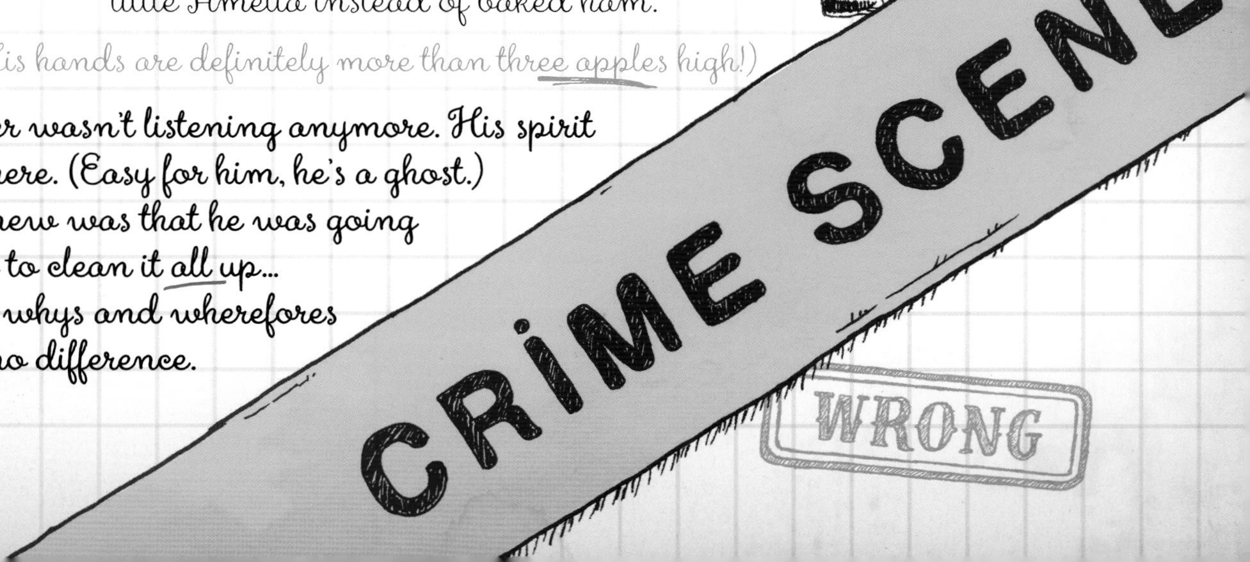
CRIME SCENE*
WRONG

= Chapter 2 =
Success, gardening, and good neighbors

Oh, the PLEASURE OF OFFERING A SCARLET BOUQUET With Love

"SNIF! SNIF!"

SUCCESS STORY AT THE INN

"I'LL BRING MY MOTHER A NICE BOUQUET OF FLOWERS. SHE'LL LIKE THAT."

—Brothers Grimm

Ever since the story of the disappearing jam got out, the inn has been completely booked. Sometimes I wonder if it isn't all part of some Machiavellian plot conjured up by my uncles to spread the word of their new inn across Fairytale Land. (Those three uncles are pretty clever.)

Now, everyone knows they have to reserve well in advance if they want to partake in the exotic ambience of the inn...

and especially if they want to try Jimmy's red berry jam.

There's even a rumor that the sixth season of "I have a monster stuck under my tongue," the hit Fairytale Land web series, is going to be shot here!!

(Maybe, with a bit of luck, I'll get a part.)

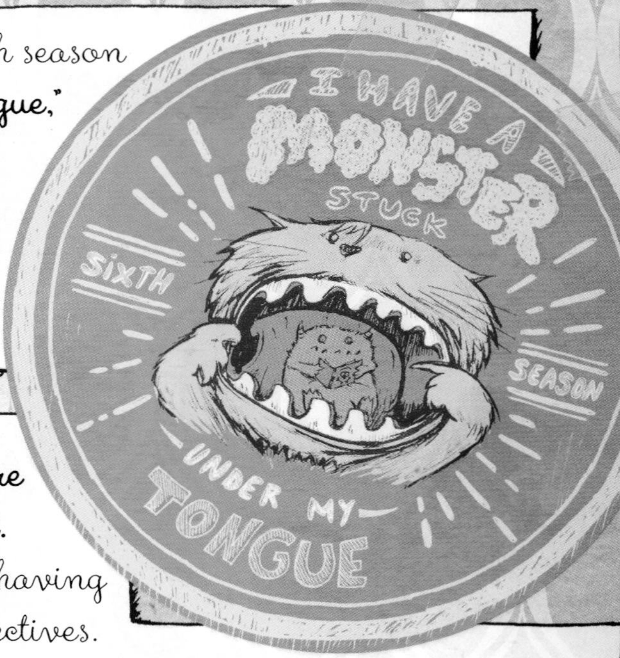
I HAVE A MONSTER STUCK UNDER MY TONGUE
SIXTH SEASON

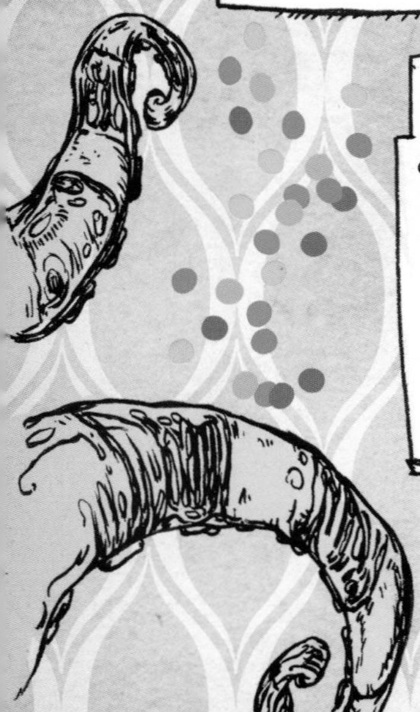

But things for Mister Nightmare and Mister Franklin aren't as great. They're having trouble getting over having been accused of theft by our two detectives. They now carry jars of red jam and home baked sliced bread (unionized) with them everywhere they go to avoid any further suspicion. And as soon as they run out of jam, they run and get more. (Smart)

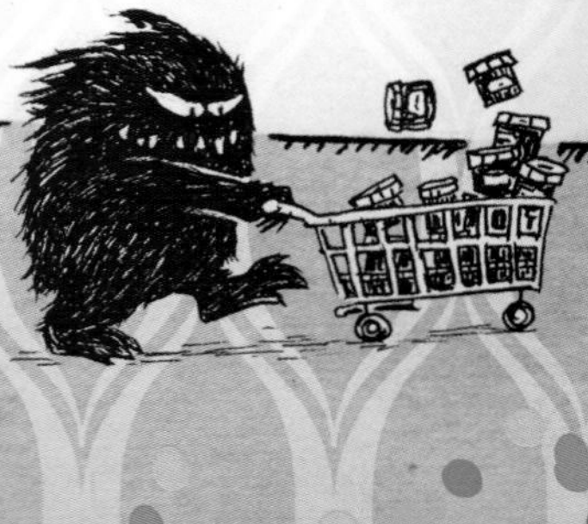

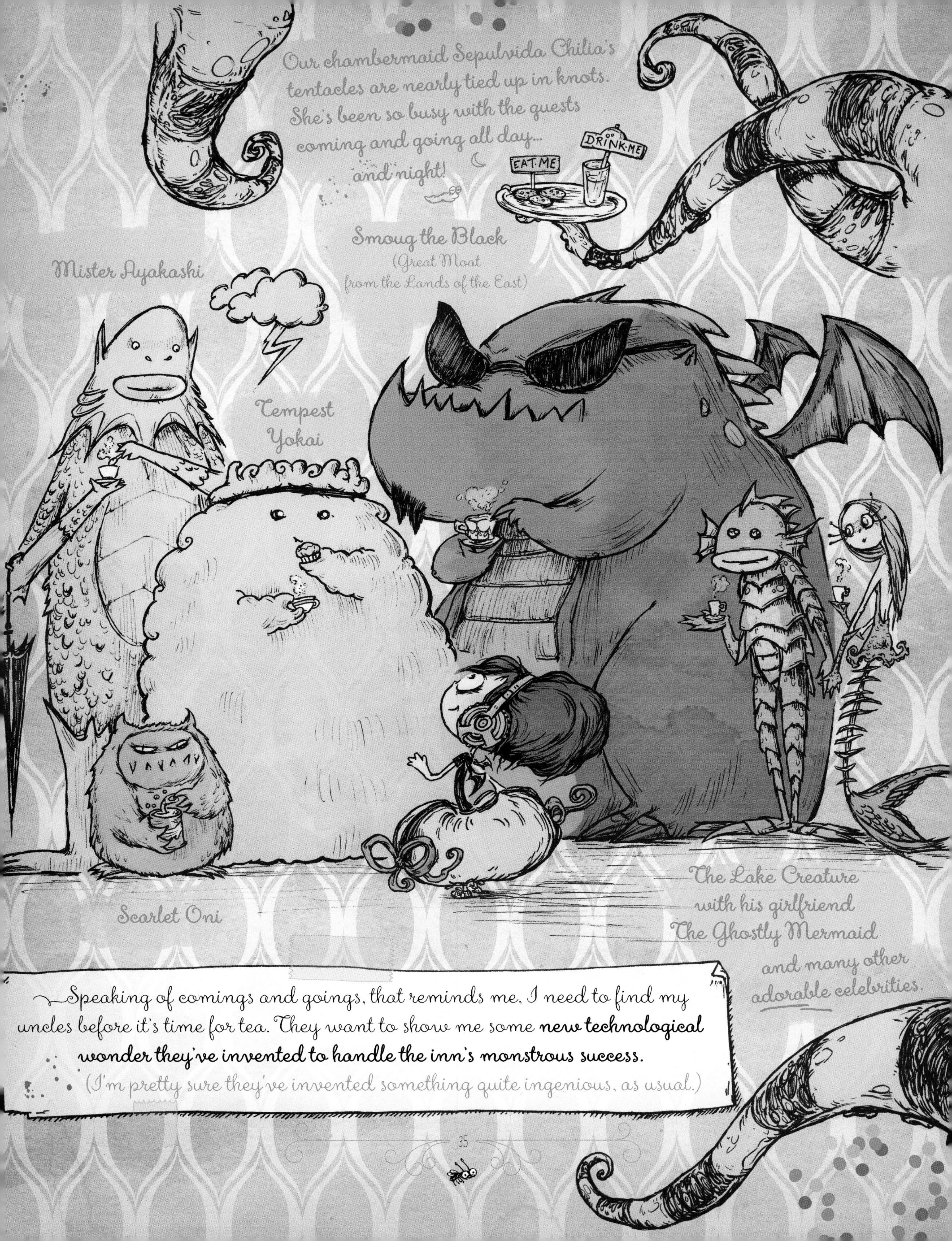

Our chambermaid Sepulvida Chilia's tentacles are nearly tied up in knots. She's been so busy with the guests coming and going all day... and night!
DRINK·ME
EAT·ME
Smoug the Black
(Great Moat
from the Lands of the East)
Mister Ayakashi
Tempest
Yokai
Scarlet Oni
The Lake Creature
with his girlfriend
The Ghostly Mermaid
and many other
adorable celebrities.

~Speaking of comings and goings, that reminds me, I need to find my uncles before it's time for tea. They want to show me some **new technological wonder they've invented to handle the inn's monstrous success.**

(I'm pretty sure they've invented something quite ingenious, as usual.)

Yup, I was right, those pigs had a brilliant idea! They turned the old creaky elevator into an incredible gadget,

A **6-STAR CONCIERGE SERVICE!**

This thing can take care of all our guests' needs faster than two swishes of a spreading knife!

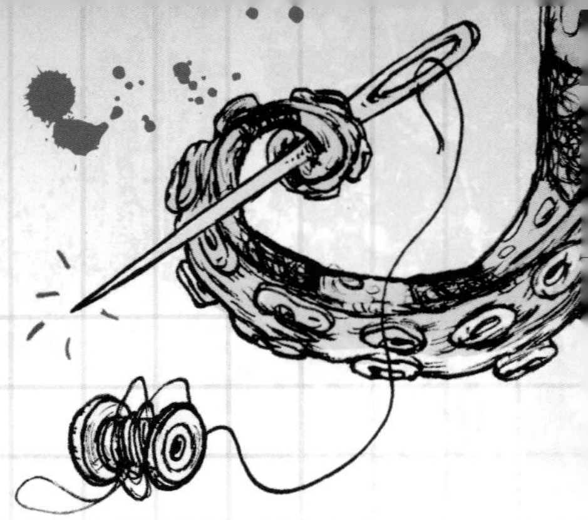

A special request?

Your fitted suit too tight?

Slide the sign under the door, and we'll take care of it for you.

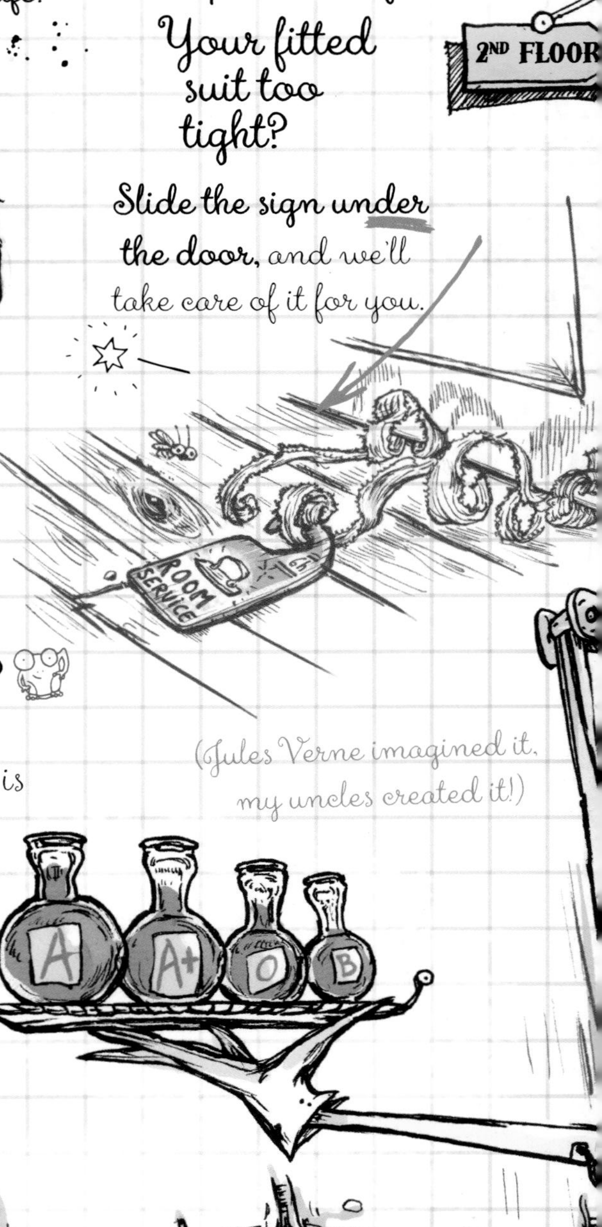
2ND FLOOR
ROOM SERVICE
A
A+
O
B

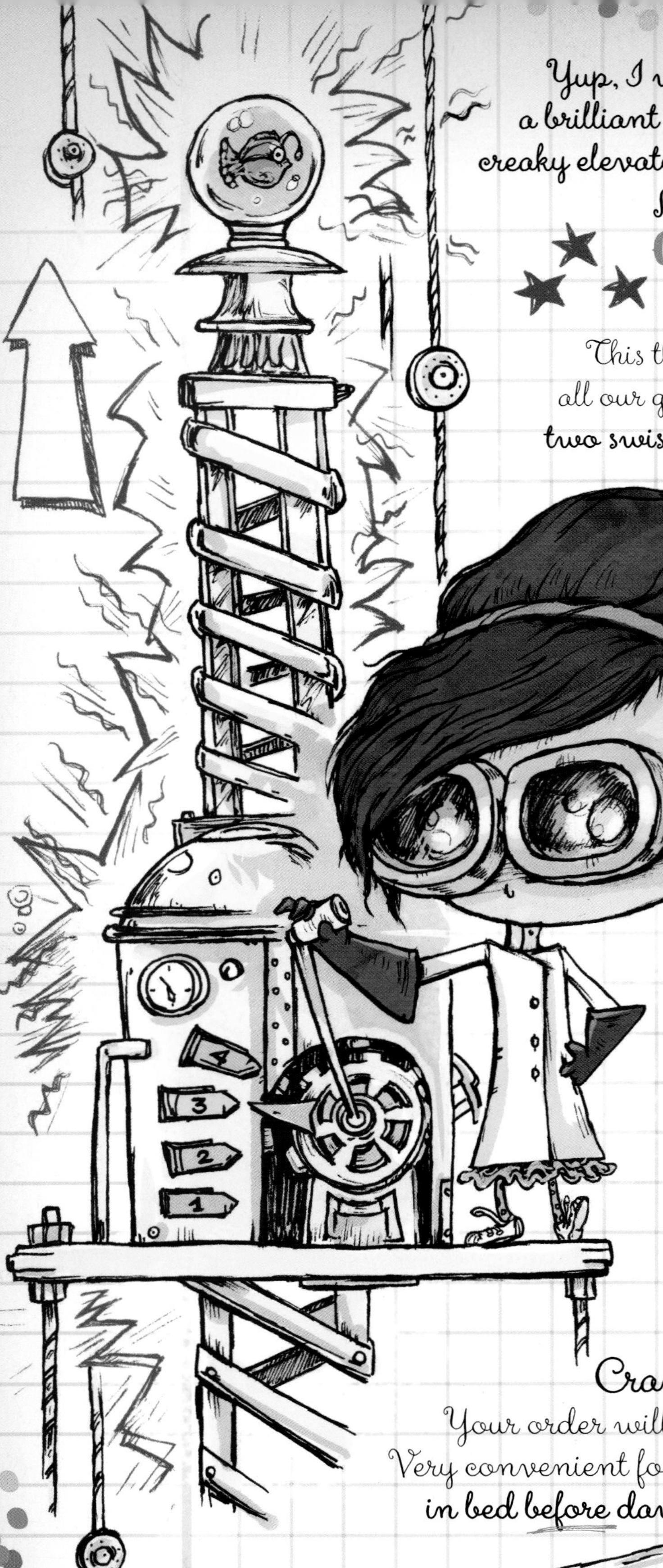
4
3
2
1

A special wish?

Just pull the lever

And our concierge is at your service!

(Jules Verne imagined it, my uncles created it!)

Craving a snack?

Your order will come lickety split. Very convenient for those that must be in bed before dawn...

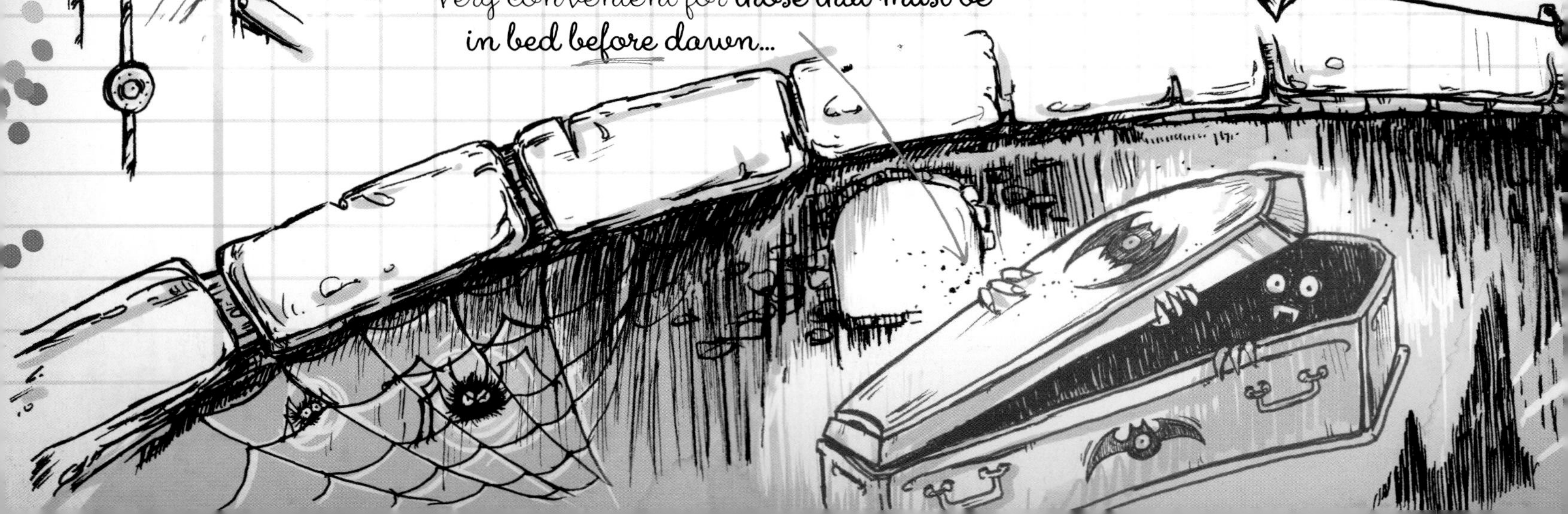

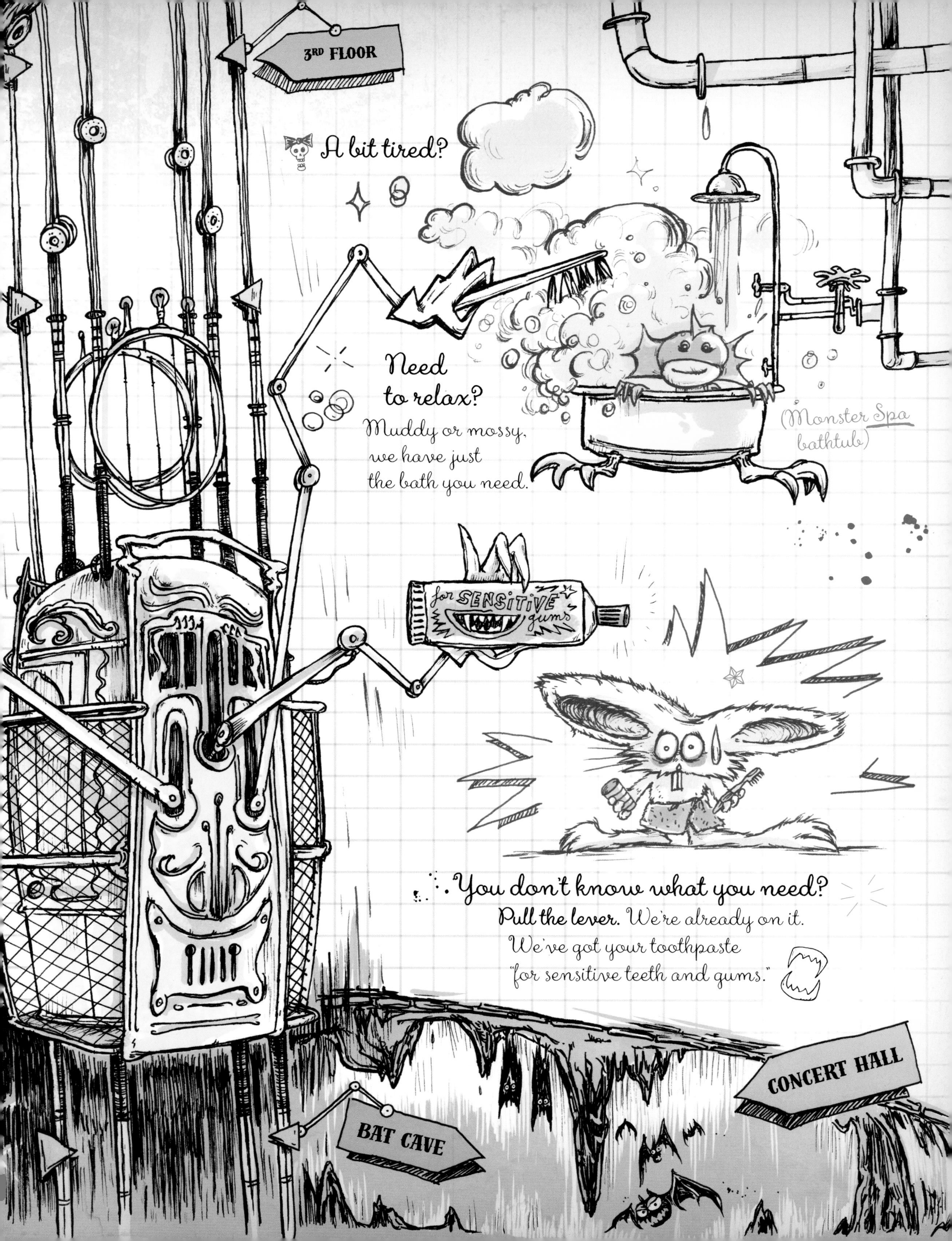
3RD FLOOR
(Monster Spa bathtub)
for SENSITIVE gums
CONCERT HALL
BAT CAVE

A bit tired?

Need to relax?

Muddy or mossy,
we have just
the bath you need.

You don't know what you need?

Pull the lever. We're already on it.
We've got your toothpaste
"for sensitive teeth and gums."

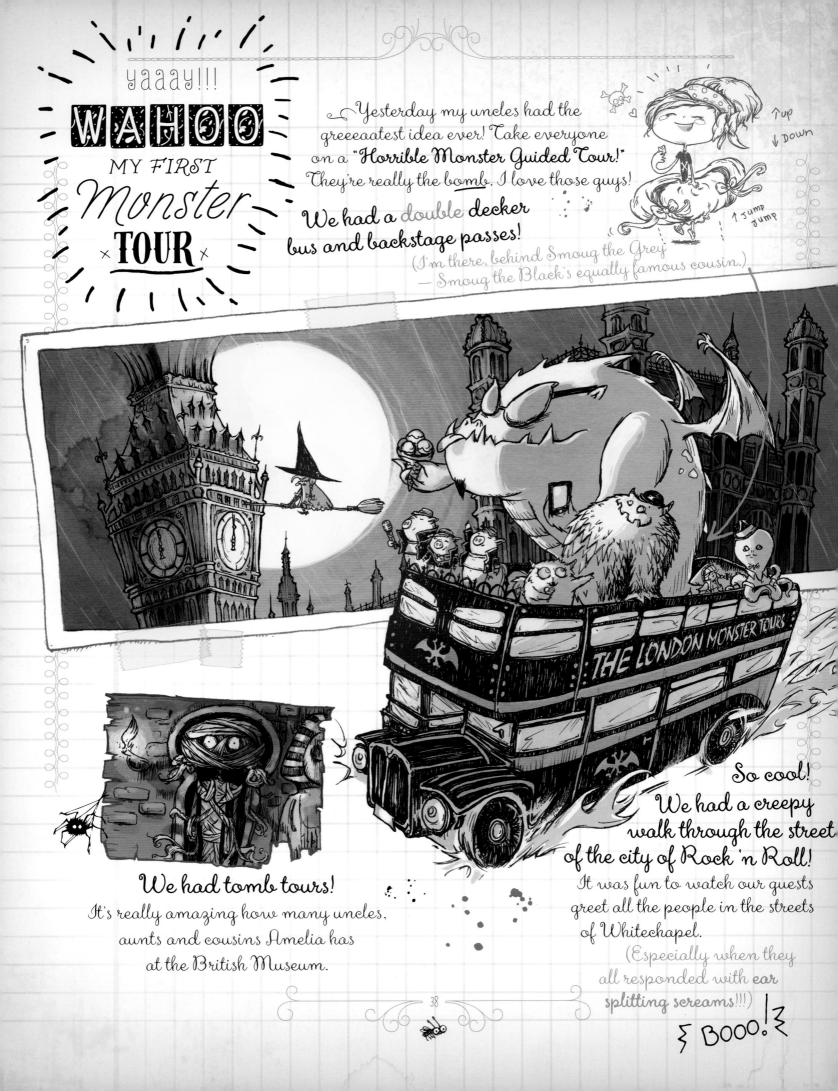

yaaay!!!

WAHOO MY FIRST *Monster* TOUR

Yesterday my uncles had the greeeaatest idea ever! Take everyone on a **"Horrible Monster Guided Tour!"** They're really the bomb. I love those guys!

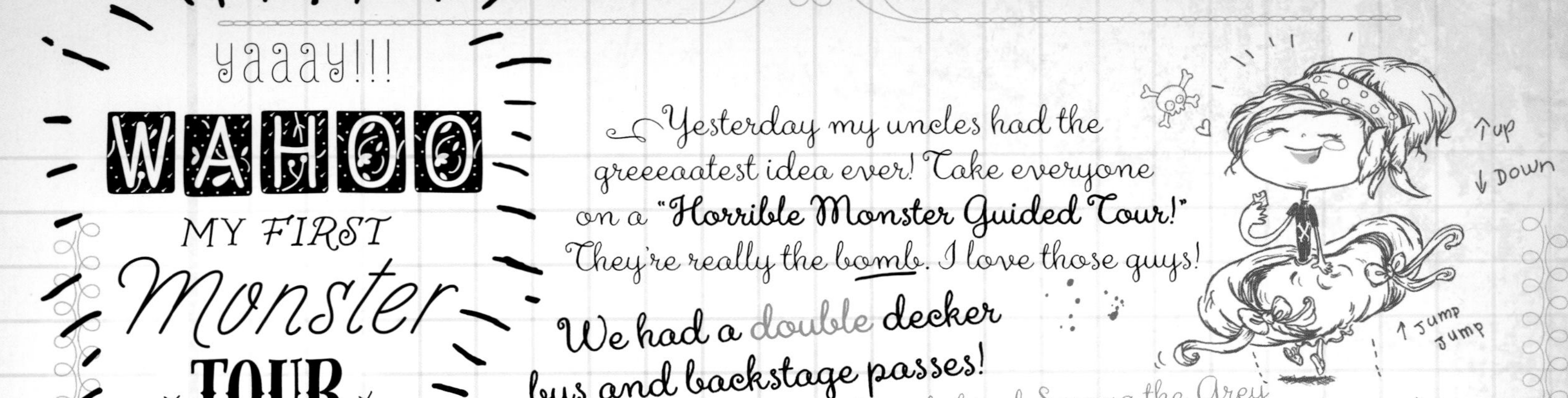
↑ up
↓ Down
↑ Jump Jump

We had a double decker bus and backstage passes!

(I'm there, behind Smoug the Grey — Smoug the Black's equally famous cousin.)

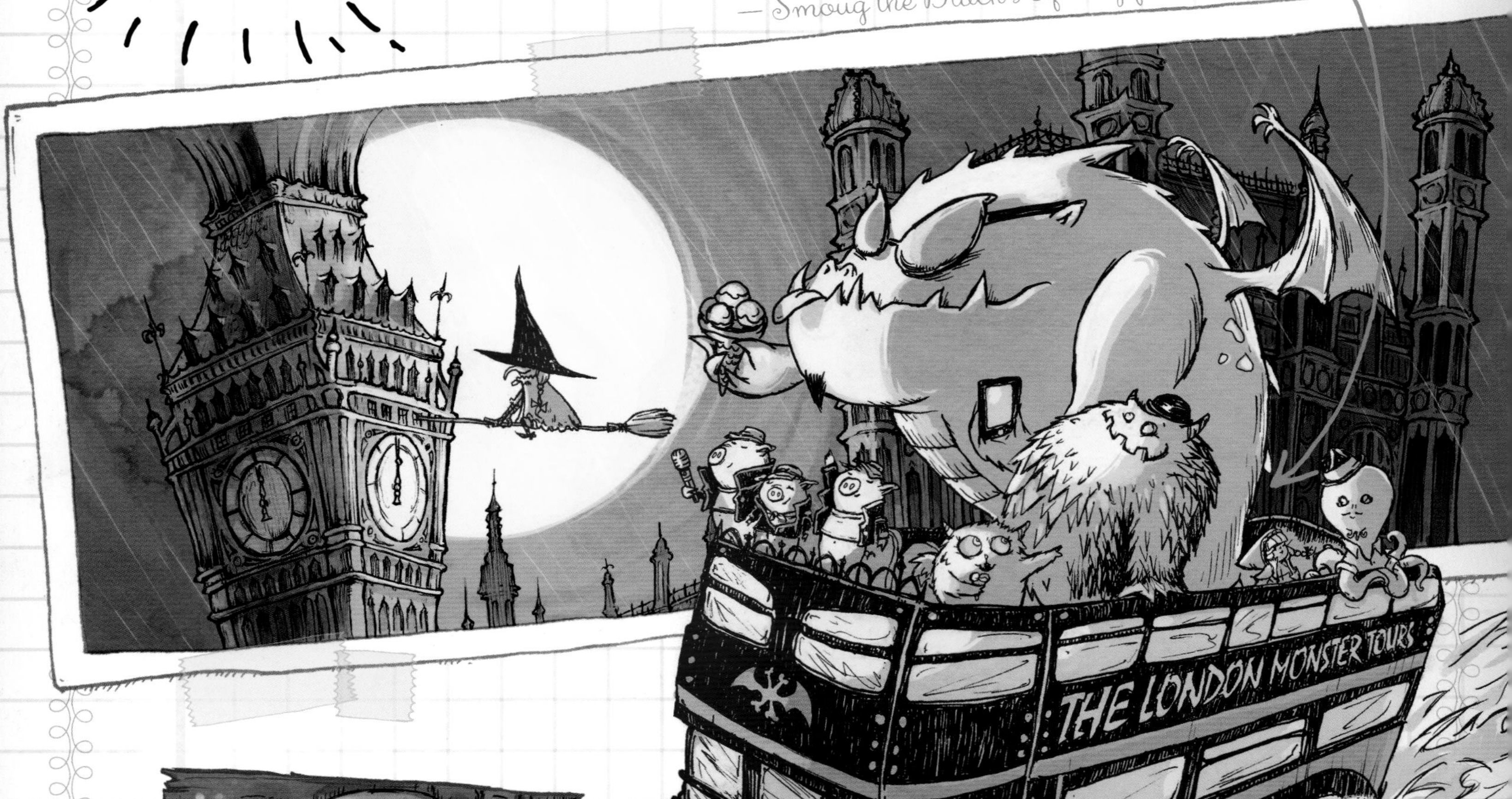
THE LONDON MONSTER TOURS

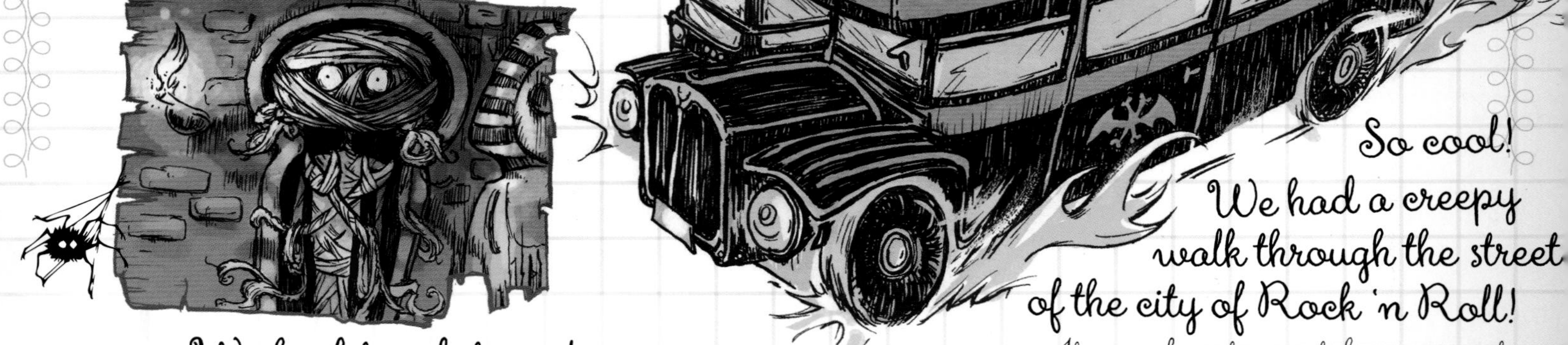

We had tomb tours!

It's really amazing how many uncles, aunts and cousins Amelia has at the British Museum.

So cool! We had a creepy walk through the street of the city of Rock 'n Roll!

It was fun to watch our guests greet all the people in the streets of Whitechapel.

(Especially when they all responded with **ear splitting screams**!!!)

BOOO!

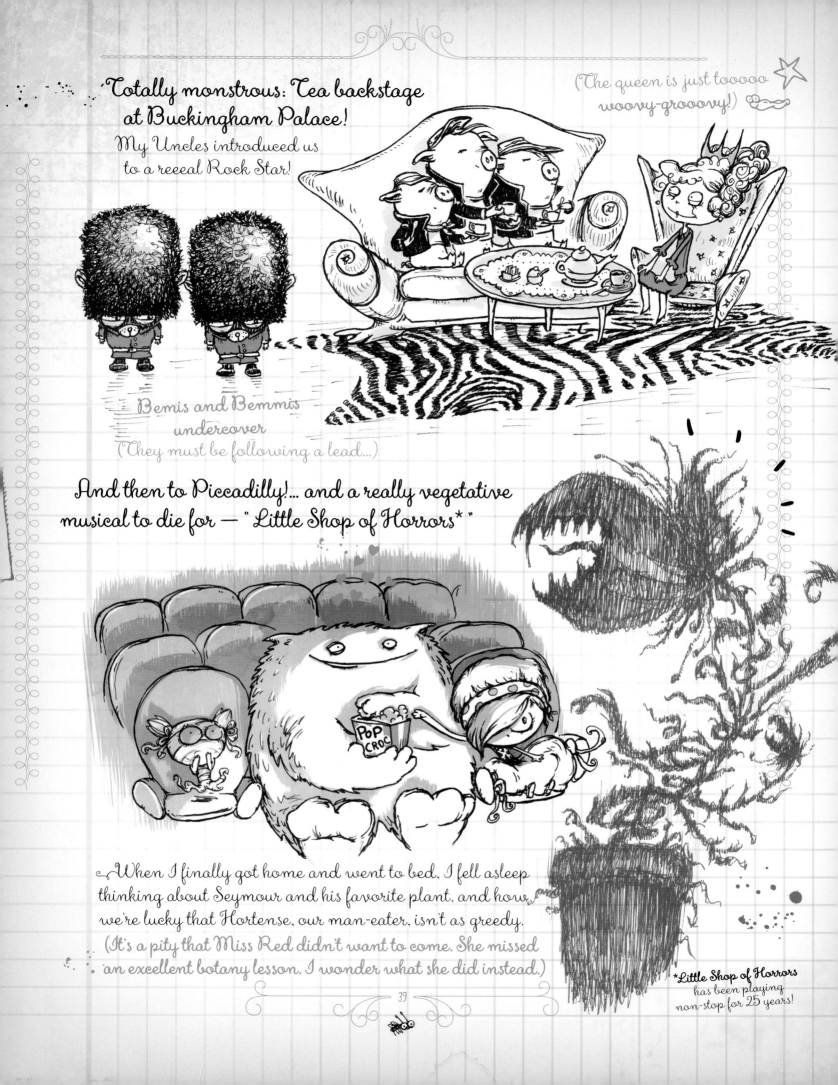

Totally monstrous: Tea backstage at Buckingham Palace!

My Uncles introduced us to a reeeal Rock Star!

(The queen is just tooooo woovy-grooovy!)

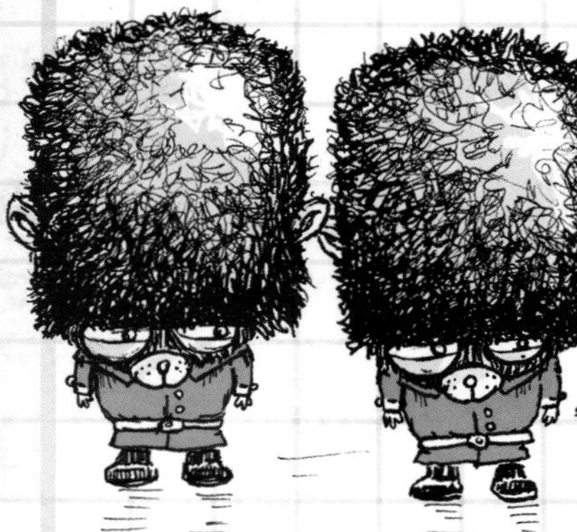

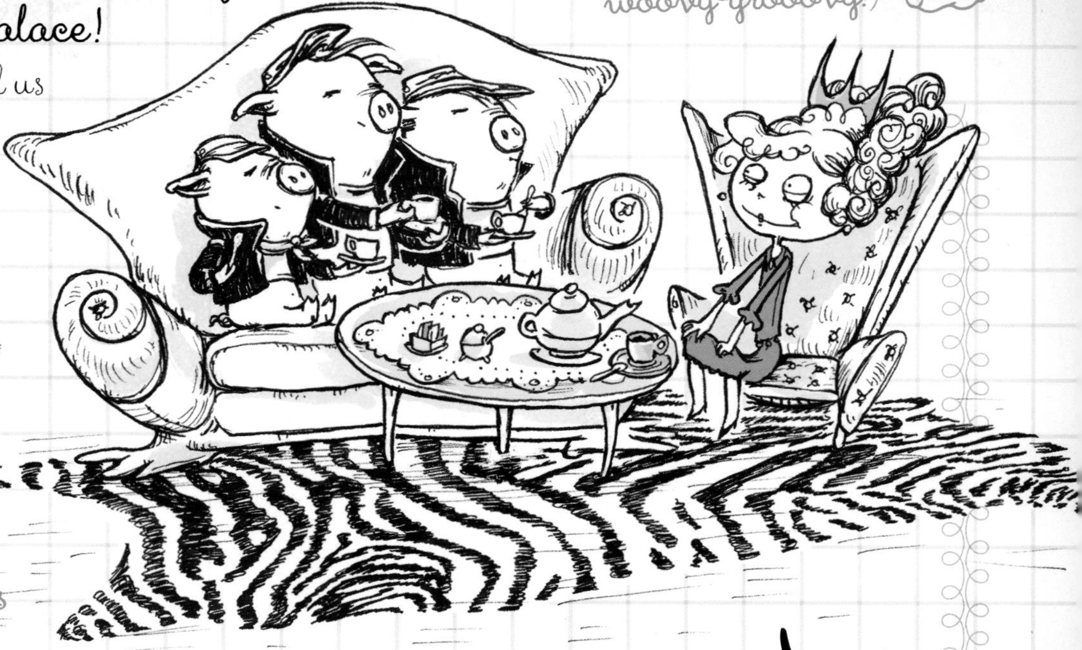

Bemis and Bemmis undercover
(They must be following a lead...)

And then to Piccadilly!... and a really vegetative musical to die for — "Little Shop of Horrors*"

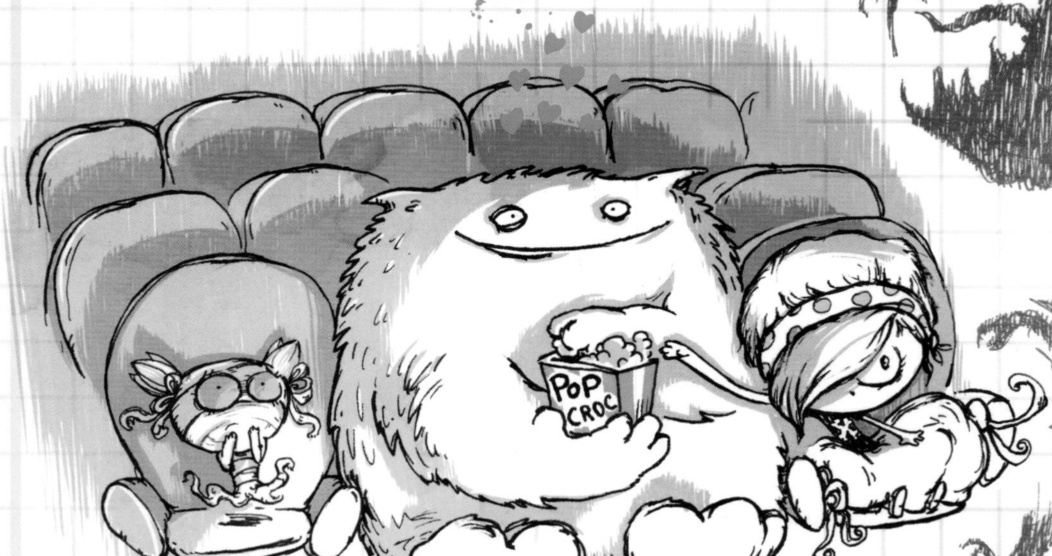
POP
CROC

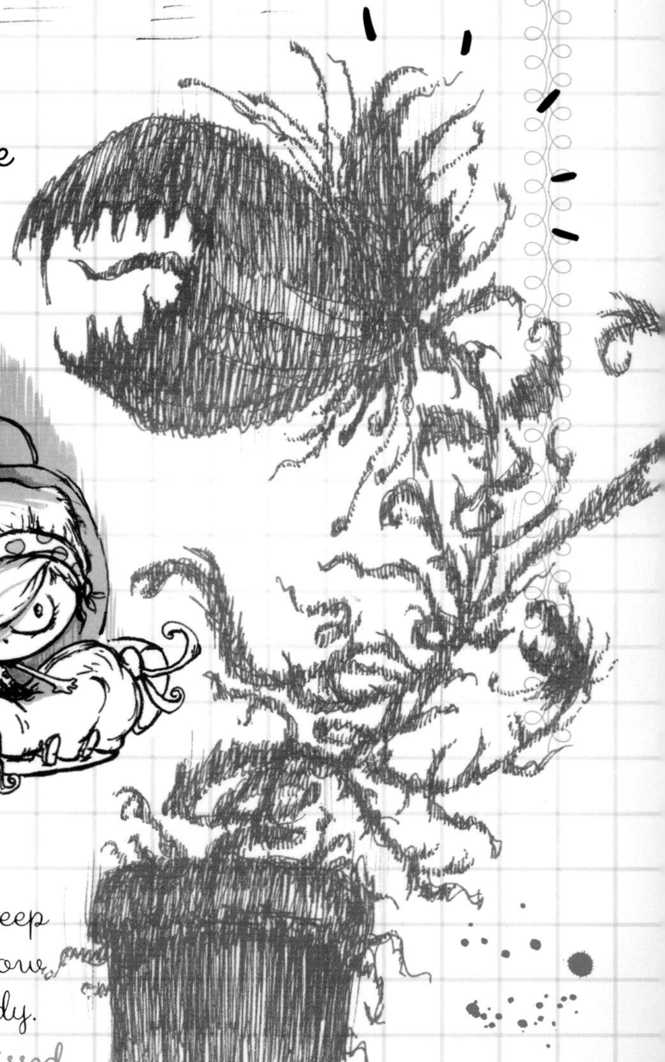

When I finally got home and went to bed, I fell asleep thinking about Seymour and his favorite plant, and how we're lucky that Hortense, our man-eater, isn't as greedy. (It's a pity that Miss Red didn't want to come. She missed an excellent botany lesson. I wonder what she did instead.)

*Little Shop of Horrors has been playing non-stop for 25 years!

The next MORNING AT BREAKFAST

Cutterrrrsss!!!!

"Cutters!" Hortense screeched loudly, rattling us in the most shocking manner **while we were at breakfast.**

Someone had clipped the heads off two of her youngest plants whose buds had come out just in time for the Grantham County horticultural beauty pageant. That must have hurt... Ouch!

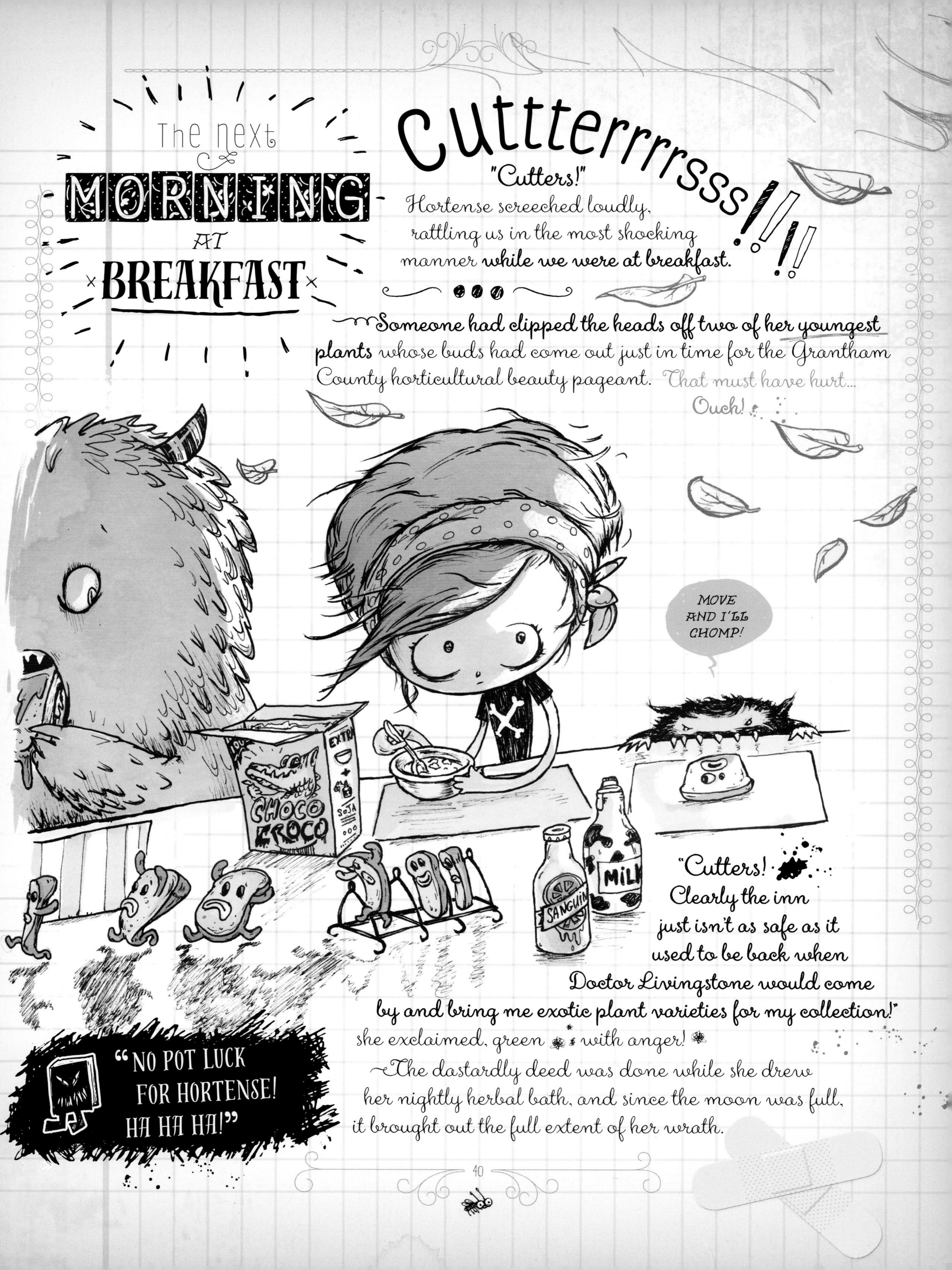

MOVE AND I'LL CHOMP!
EXTRA
CHOCO CROCO
SOJA
SANGUIN
MILK

"Cutters! Clearly the inn just isn't as safe as it used to be back when Doctor Livingstone would come by and bring me exotic plant varieties for my collection!" she exclaimed, green with anger!

The dastardly deed was done while she drew her nightly herbal bath, and since the moon was full, it brought out the full extent of her wrath.

"NO POT LUCK FOR HORTENSE! HA HA HA!"

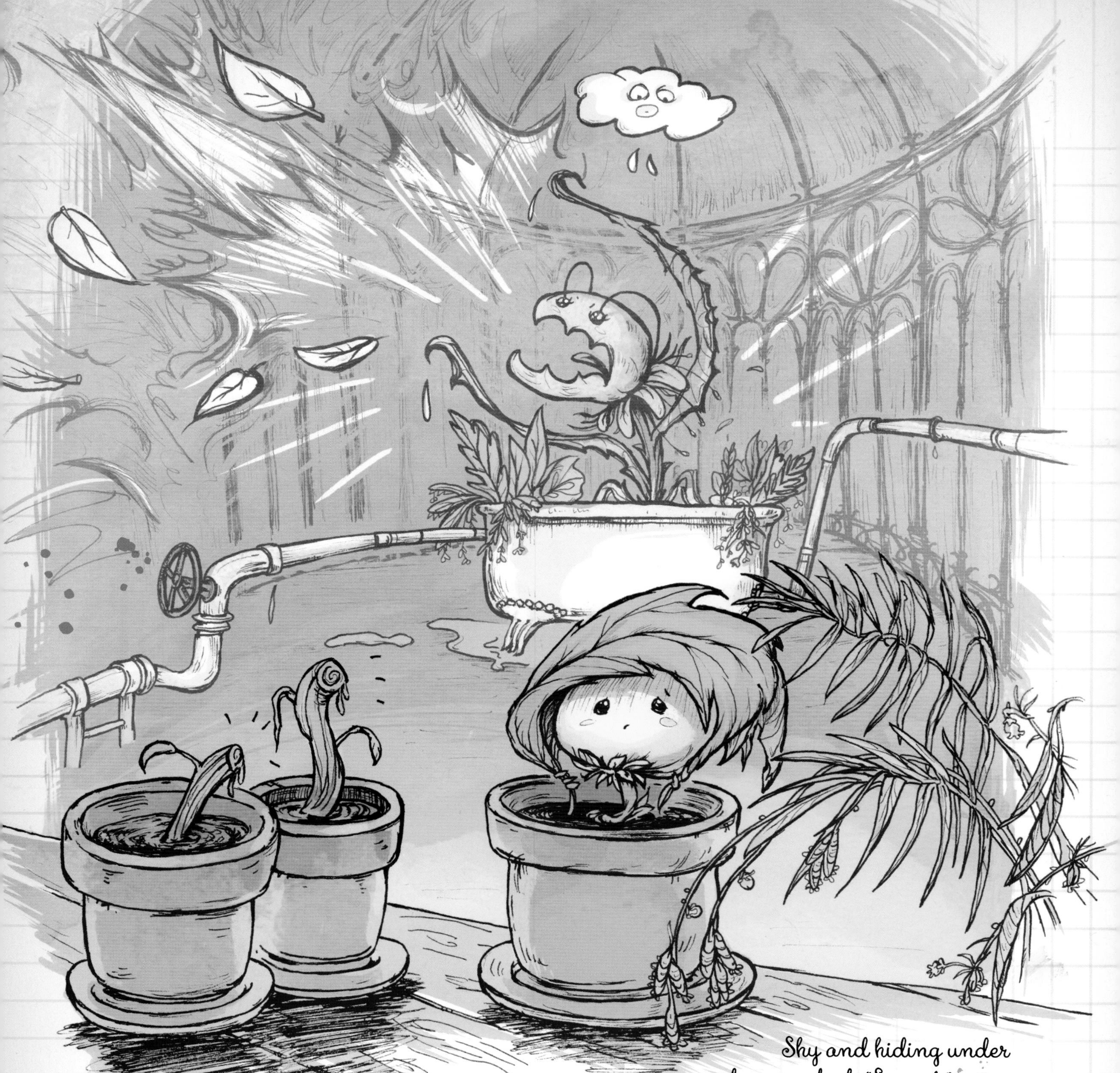

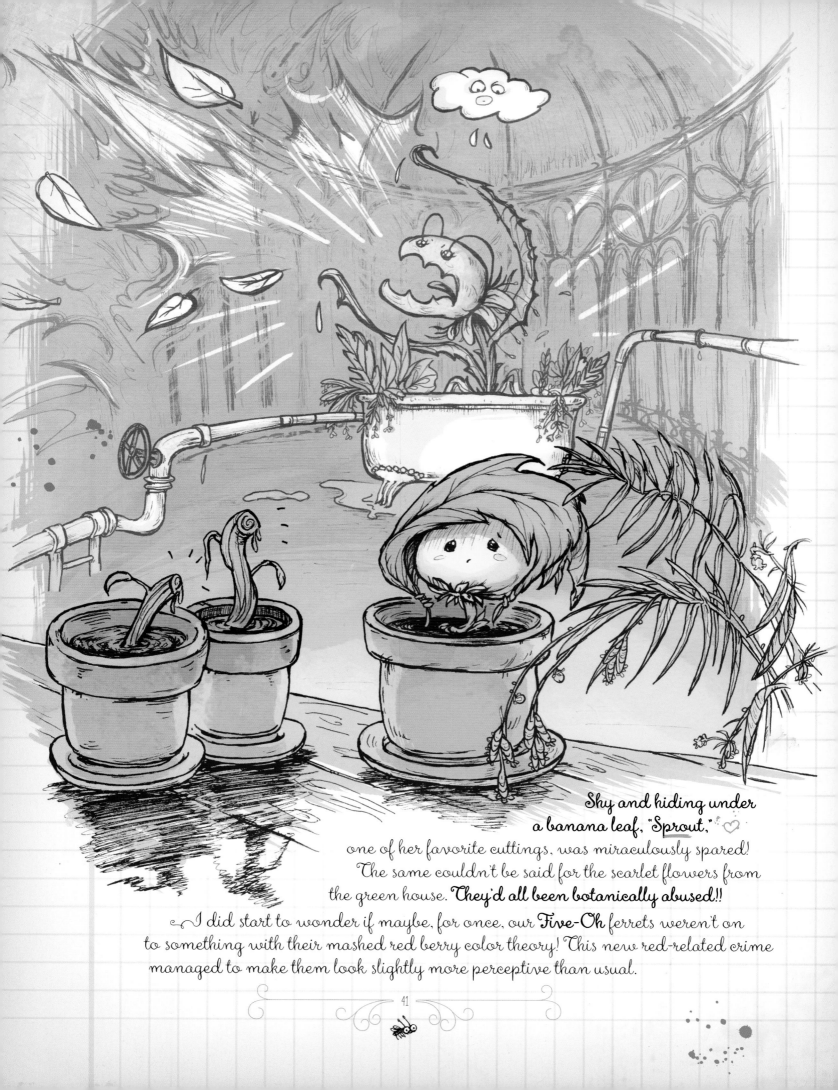

Shy and hiding under a banana leaf, "Sprout," ♡ one of her favorite cuttings, was miraculously spared! The same couldn't be said for the scarlet flowers from the green house. **They'd all been botanically abused!!**

I did start to wonder if maybe, for once, our **Five-Oh** ferrets weren't on to something with their mashed red berry color theory! This new red-related crime managed to make them look slightly more perceptive than usual.

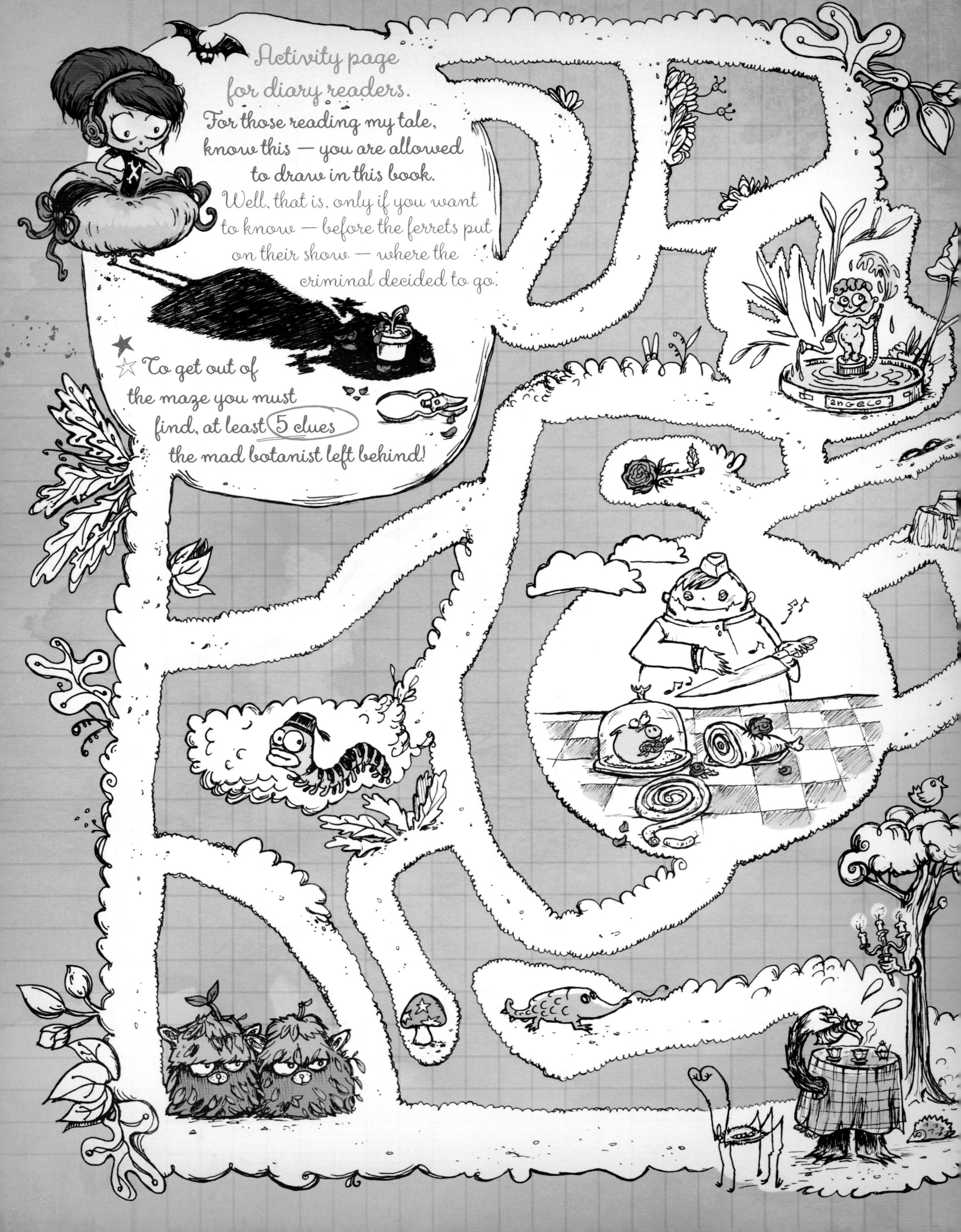
Activity page for diary readers.
For those reading my tale, know this — you are allowed to draw in this book.
Well, that is, only if you want to know — before the ferrets put on their show — where the criminal decided to go.
☆ To get out of the maze you must find, at least 5 clues the mad botanist left behind!
angelo

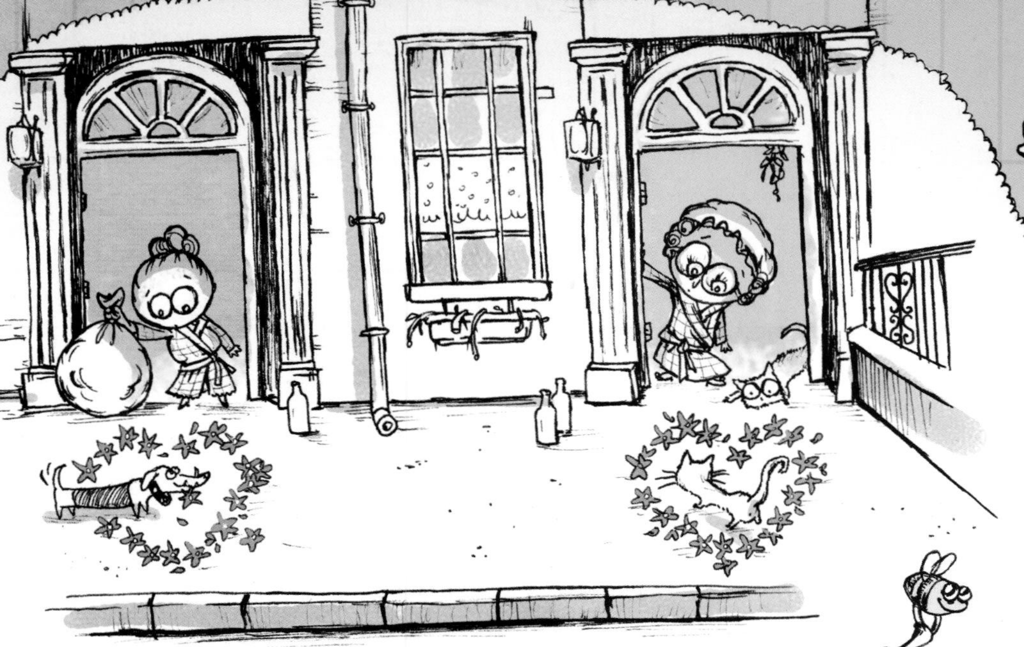

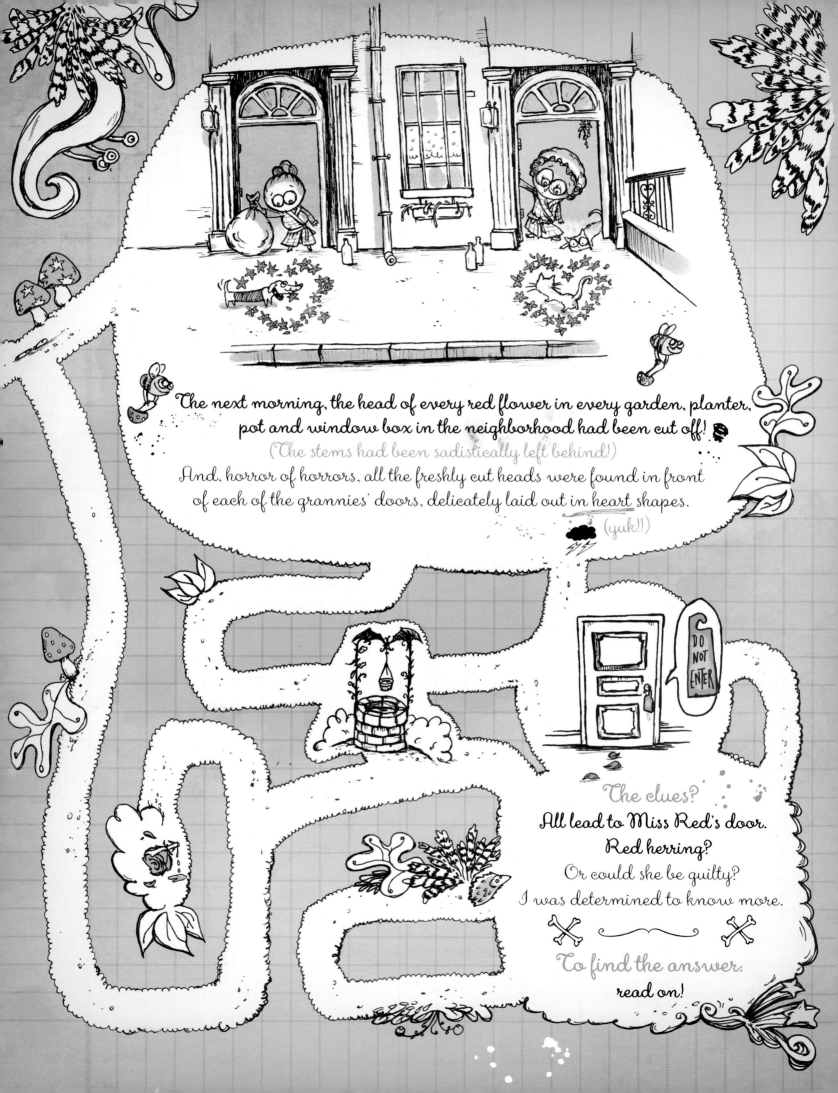

The next morning, the head of every red flower in every garden, planter, pot and window box in the neighborhood had been cut off!

(The stems had been sadistically left behind!)

And, horror of horrors, all the freshly cut heads were found in front of each of the grannies' doors, delicately laid out in heart shapes.

(yuk!!)

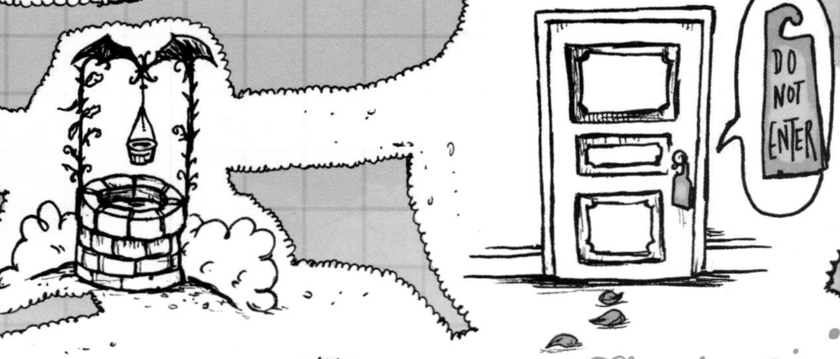
DO NOT ENTER

The clues?

All lead to Miss Red's door.

Red herring?

Or could she be guilty?

I was determined to know more.

To find the answer:

read on!

While Bemis and Bemmis were still in the maze, I ran off to talk with Duster to find out how long Miss Red's door had been closed. Embarrassed, he admitted to being as puzzled by all this as I was. In fact, ever since Miss Red, "who is so pretty and cute and nice," has been here, her room has been off limits to him!

Duster experiences a quick range of emotions. He always takes things so personally!

A bit ridiculous for an upstairs ghost.

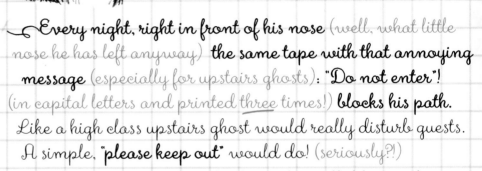

Every night, right in front of his nose (well, what little nose he has left anyway) the same tape with that annoying message (especially for upstairs ghosts): "Do not enter"! (in capital letters and printed three times!) blocks his path. Like a high class upstairs ghost would really disturb guests. A simple, "please keep out" would do! (seriously?!)

Everybody knows that a ghost only shows himself if he needs to... or if you need him. And Miss Red has never asked for anything, not even a classic late-night toe tickle while sleeping!

O NOT ENTER   DO

Without making a sound, Amelia the mummy joined us. (her sniffles never betray her presence.)

She seemed a bit more unraveled than usual, which is worrying, and made me ask why she was pulling a suitcase.

"**I'm being kept up nights,**" she said, still sniffling and pulling her bag. "**I can't take it anymore.**"

Duster asked what the problem was.

She said she was hearing voices through the walls, coming from the room next door. They kept saying the same things over and over again:

"Where are you off to so early?"
"To grandma's house!"
"Where does she live?"
"Deep in the wood!"
"What have you got in the basket?"

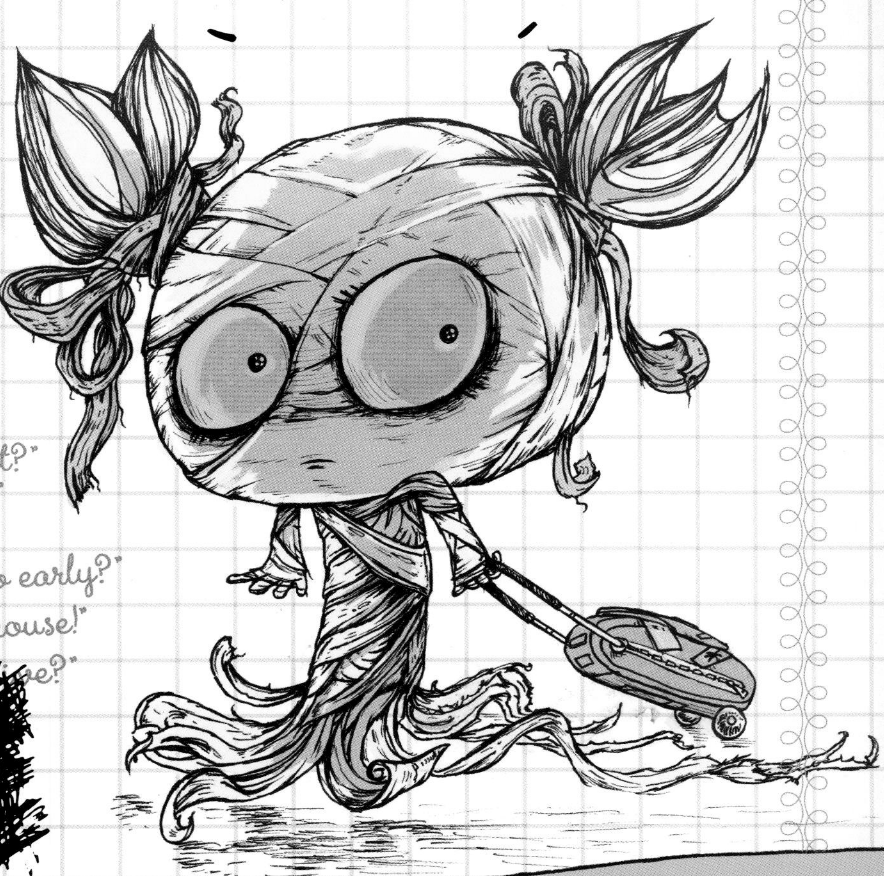

"HEY, I'VE HEARD THAT SOMEWHERE BEFORE...

...BUT IT NEVER KEPT ME UP NIGHTS!"

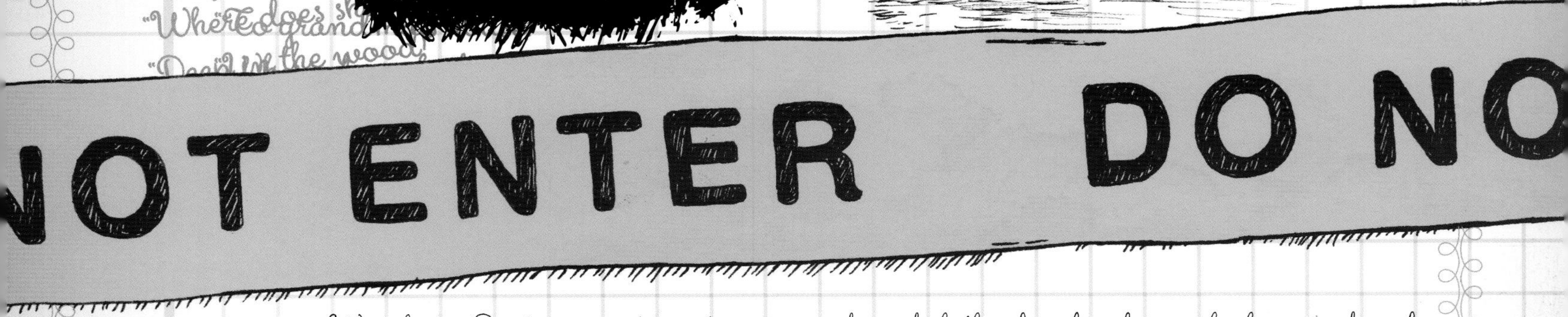
NOT ENTER DO NO

Watching Duster's reaction: to nervously polish the doorknob — which was already sparkling— I started to really lose my patience. So, I banged on the door.

A tiny but hoarse voice answered: "Please leave me alone!"

Amelia jumped as soon as she heard it, so I decided to take this opportunity to ask another question: "Is there someone in there with you?"

I got back a very soft: "No, I'm all alone..."

In a fit of panic, Amelia raced back to her room and hid.

(Hmm? I guess she doesn't want to leave anymore.)

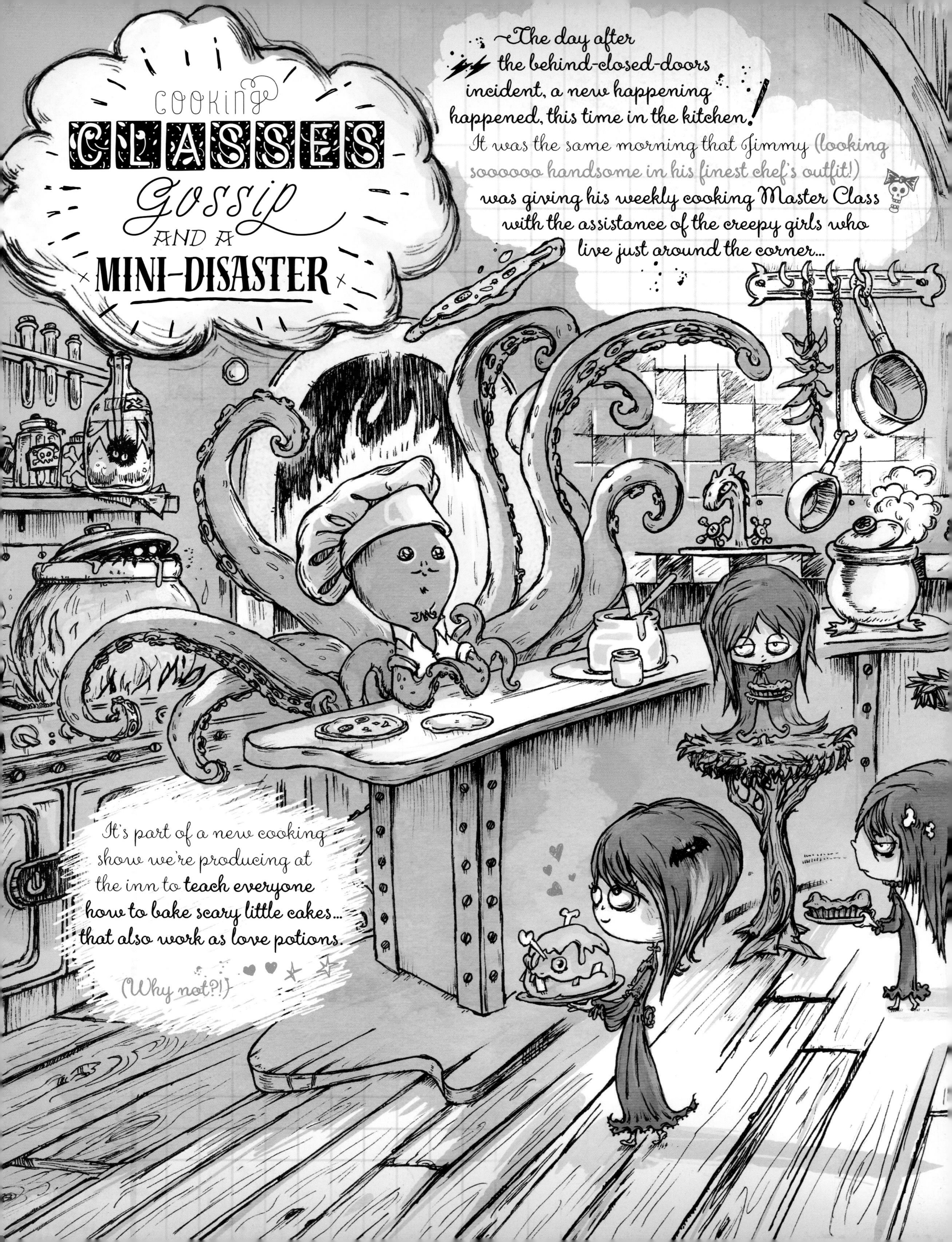

COOKING CLASSES GOSSIP AND A MINI-DISASTER
The day after the behind-closed-doors incident, a new happening happened, this time in the kitchen!
It was the same morning that Jimmy (looking soooooo handsome in his finest chef's outfit!) was giving his weekly cooking Master Class with the assistance of the creepy girls who live just around the corner...
It's part of a new cooking show we're producing at the inn to teach everyone how to bake scary little cakes... that also work as love potions.
(Why not?!)

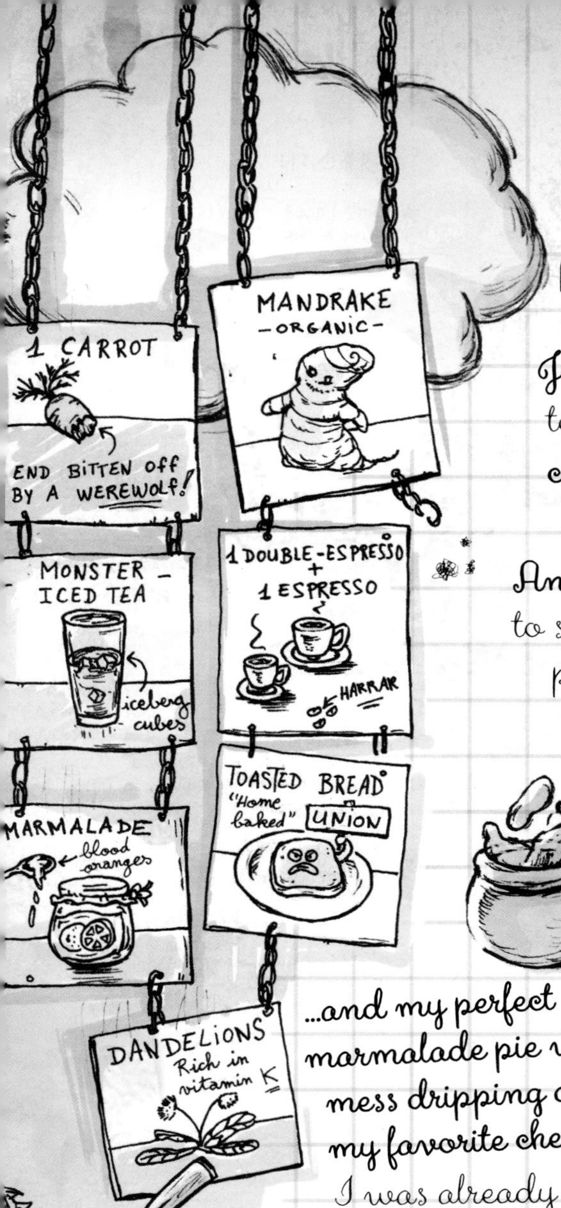
1 CARROT
END BITTEN OFF BY A WEREWOLF!
MANDRAKE
-ORGANIC-
MONSTER ICED TEA
iceberg cubes
1 DOUBLE-ESPRESSO + 1 ESPRESSO
HARRAR
MARMALADE
blood oranges
TOASTED BREAD
"Home baked"
UNION
DANDELIONS
Rich in vitamin K

I'll never forget it. It happened just as Jimmy was admiring the first creations coming out of the oven (with love) that had been prepared the night before by his fan-club (Which includes me!)...!

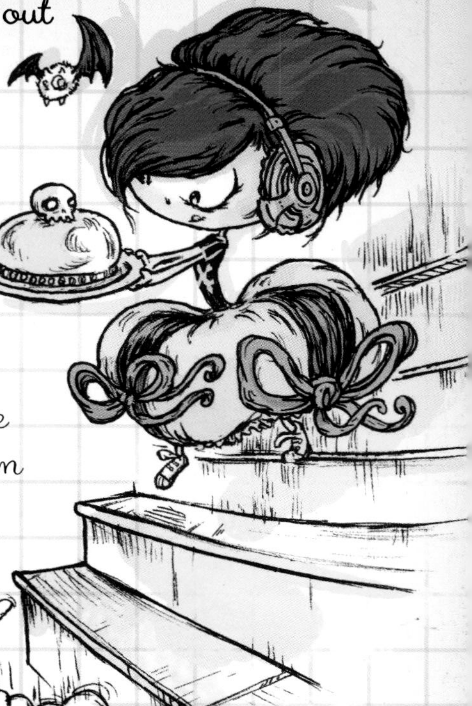

Just as I was coming down the stairs to the kitchen, proudly (and carefully) carrying my delicious marmalade pie (especially "lover sweet")!

And just as Duster decided to come find me to say that more "Do not enter" tape had been put up in front of Miss Red's door...

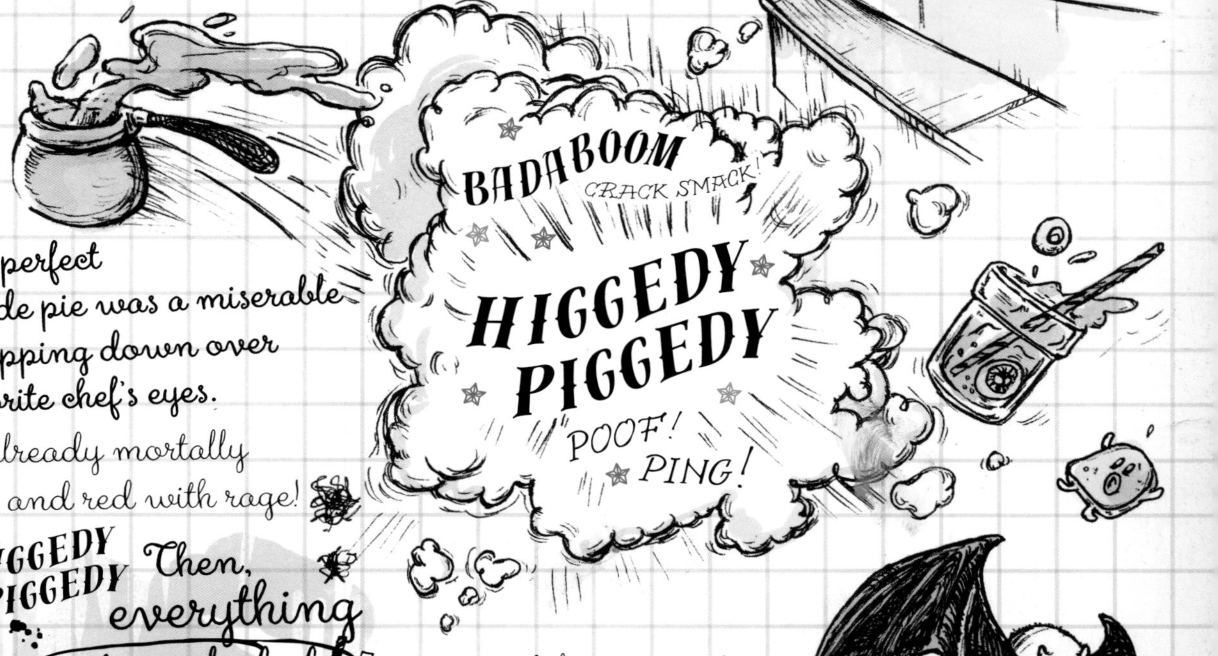
BADABOOM
CRACK SMACK!
HIGGEDY PIGGEDY
POOF!
PING!

...and my perfect marmalade pie was a miserable mess dripping down over my favorite chef's eyes.

I was already mortally mortified and red with rage!

HIGGEDY PIGGEDY Then, everything just exploded!?

Guess why?!...

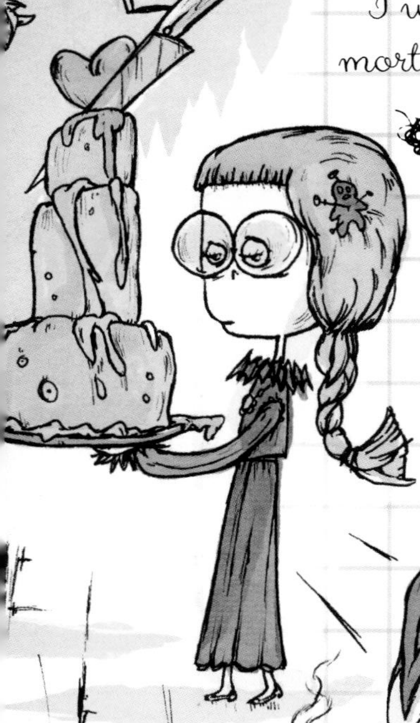

Dandelion scones, mandrake muffins, vinegar layer cake...

...even the "four incantation" pizza Jimmy had made, thanking us for coming ...

(what a sweetheart) ♡

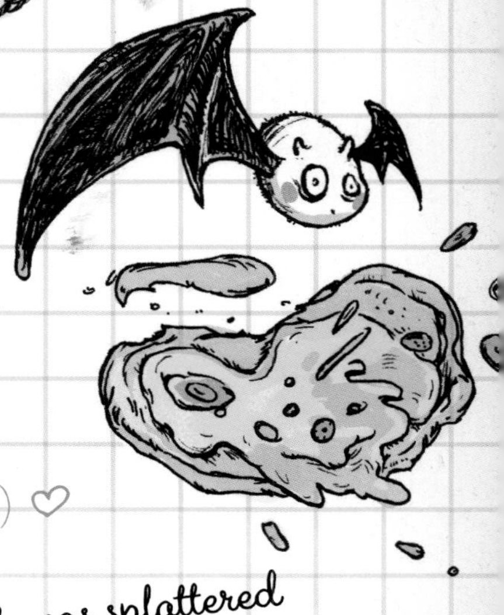

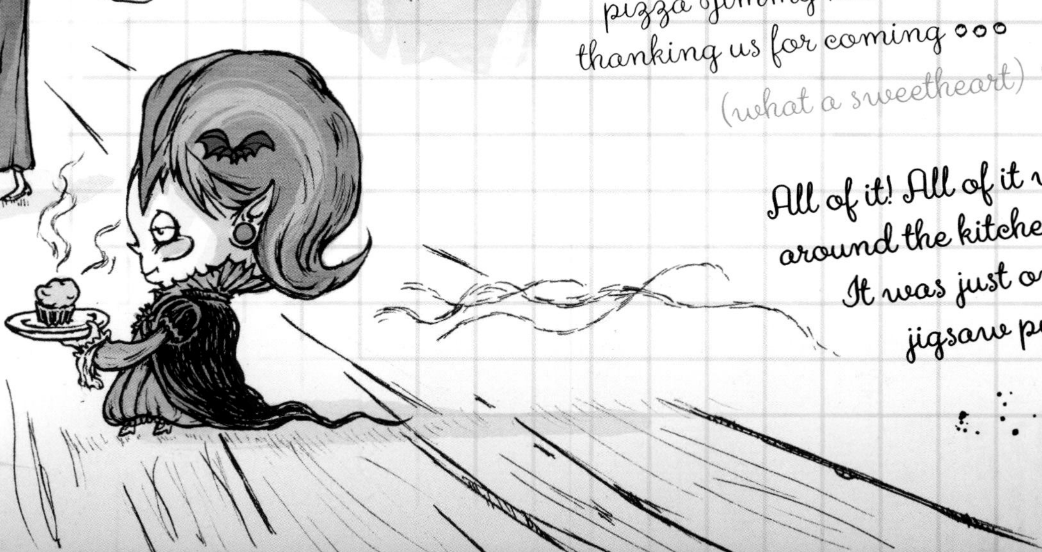

All of it! All of it was splattered around the kitchen in little pieces. It was just one mega-messy jigsaw puzzle!!!

HOW to MANAGE AN UPSTAIRS ghost

Chaaaooooooosss!!!!

Enough! Enough!
This is getting out of hand!

Everyone comes to see monsters and go sightseeing!
Not to spend time locked up behind closed doors or have marmalade drip off our heads!

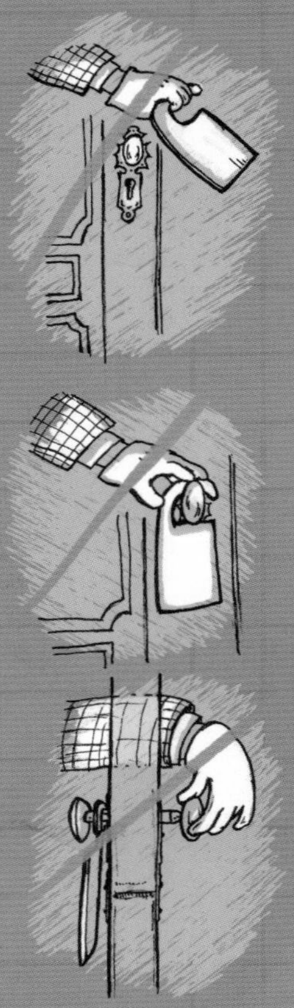

"Cataclysmic chaos! Duster, go take a look inside the room... It's easy for you. You are a ghost, after all, aren't you?!" I said to Duster, who turned as gray as a shroud that had spent too much time in some catacomb or another.

I'm not sure if he was still a bit upset about the kitchen incident or if he was just offended by my suggestion, but he said:

"The rules of conduct for top level inn staff quite clearly state that ghost personnel may not, under any circumstances, take off, move, or ignore any no entry indications. The guest is king!"

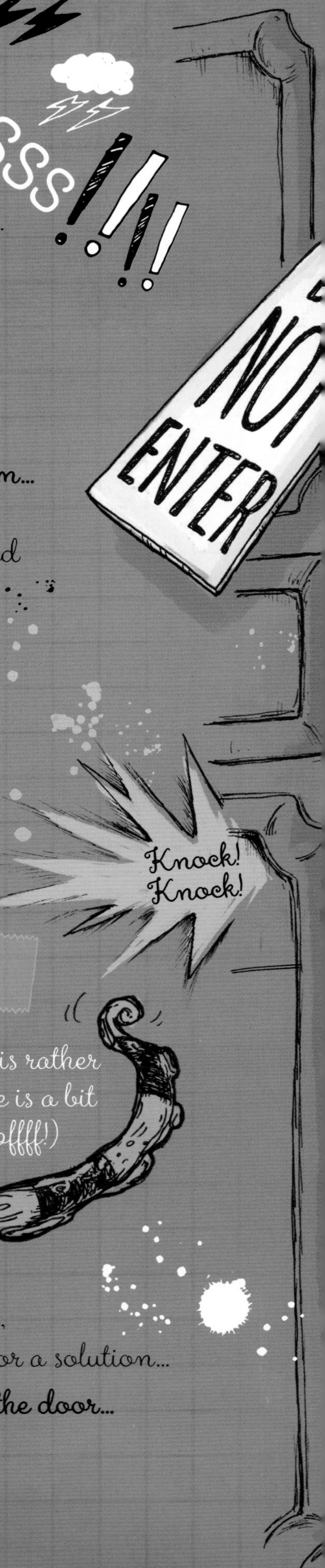
NOT ENTER
Knock! Knock!

(Actually, despite his rather laid back demeanor, he is a bit of a fuddy-duddy... pffff!)

Having heard my exchange with Duster, Sepulvida Chilias, always hoping to give a helping hand, (well, you know what I mean), decided to discreetly try for a solution...

Unrolling one of her tentacles, she knocked on the door...

"Who is it?" murmured a little voice.
I answered with:
- "Is everything okay, Miss Red?"
...no answer...and then, once again you could hear the little voices in conversation behind the door:
"Where are you off to so early?"
"To grandma's house!"
"But that's really far!"
"No, it's close! I think I'll bring her something to eat."

I quickly said:
-"Uh, probably not, the kitchen kinda blew up!"
And the voice — pretending to be hoarse — answered:
-"Oh, then how about a frozen meal?"
(Now that threw me for a loop. I wasn't sure what to say.)

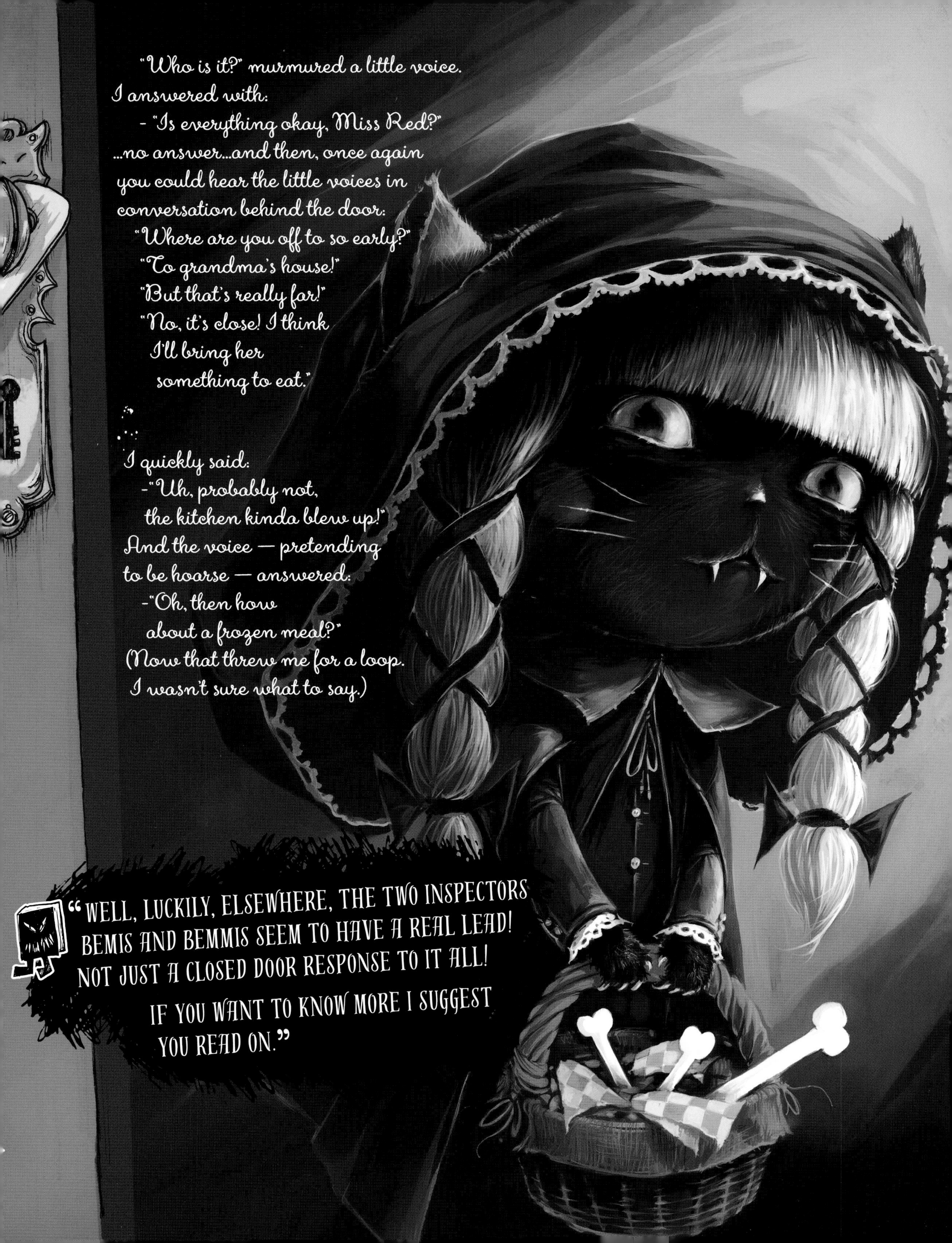

"WELL, LUCKILY, ELSEWHERE, THE TWO INSPECTORS BEMIS AND BEMMIS SEEM TO HAVE A REAL LEAD! NOT JUST A CLOSED DOOR RESPONSE TO IT ALL!

IF YOU WANT TO KNOW MORE I SUGGEST YOU READ ON."

Chapter 3
Rumpus rock and spiced pie

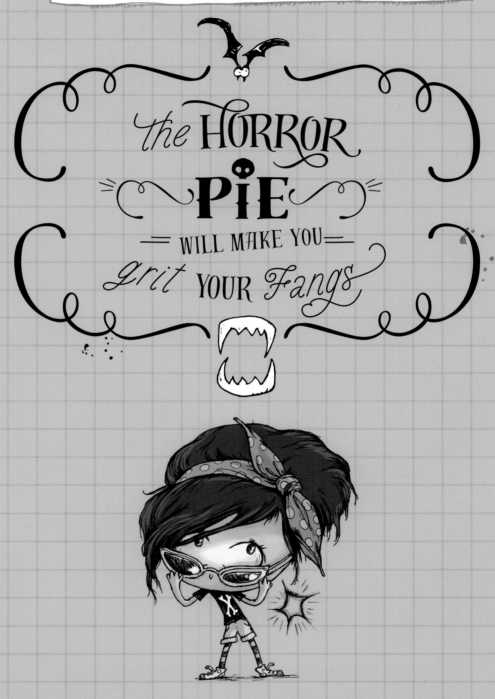

the HORROR PIE WILL MAKE YOU grit YOUR Fangs

“‘OH! BUT GRANDMOTHER,
WHAT A TERRIBLE BIG MOUTH YOU HAVE!’
‘ALL THE BETTER TO EAT YOU WITH, MY DEAR!’”

Brothers Grimm

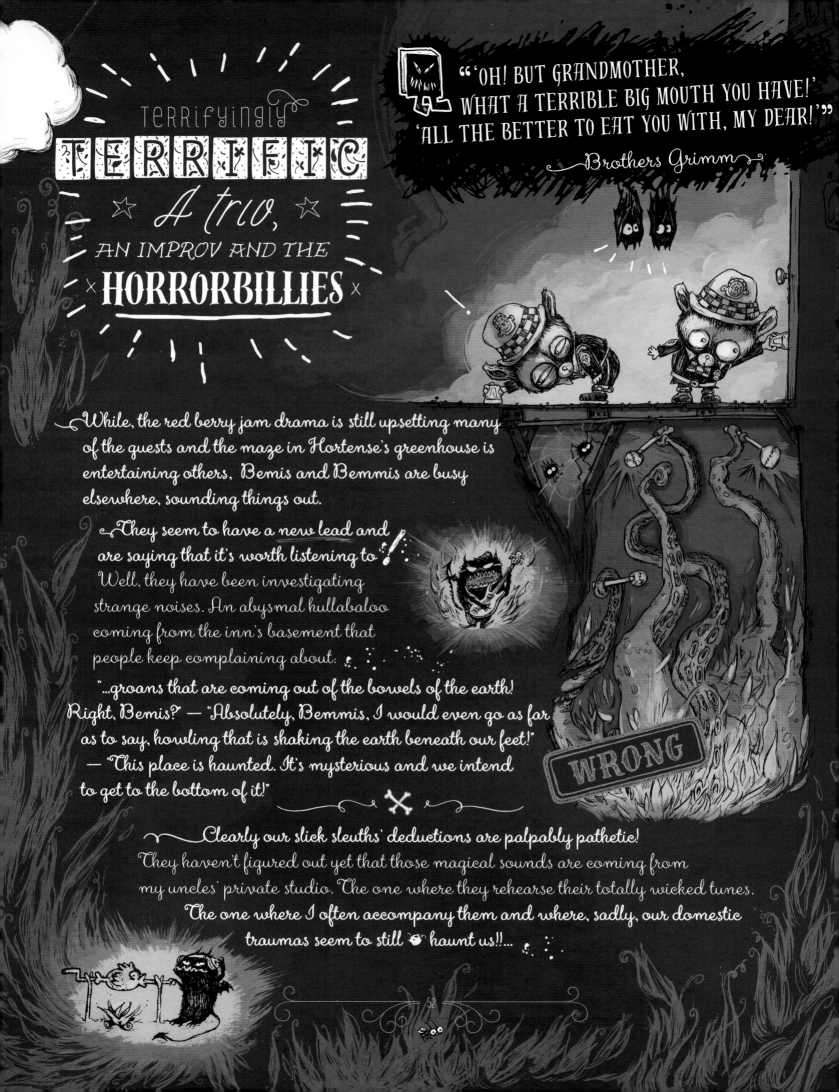

Terrifyingly TERRIFIC A trio, an improv and the HORRORBILLIES

WRONG

While, the red berry jam drama is still upsetting many of the guests and the maze in Hortense's greenhouse is entertaining others, Bemis and Bemmis are busy elsewhere, sounding things out.

They seem to have a new lead and are saying that it's worth listening to! Well, they have been investigating strange noises. An abysmal hullabaloo coming from the inn's basement that people keep complaining about:

"...groans that are coming out of the bowels of the earth! Right, Bemis?" — "Absolutely, Bemmis, I would even go as far as to say, howling that is shaking the earth beneath our feet!" — "This place is haunted. It's mysterious and we intend to get to the bottom of it!"

Clearly our slick sleuths' deductions are palpably pathetic! They haven't figured out yet that those magical sounds are coming from my uncles' private studio. The one where they rehearse their totally wicked tunes. The one where I often accompany them and where, sadly, our domestic traumas seem to still haunt us!!...

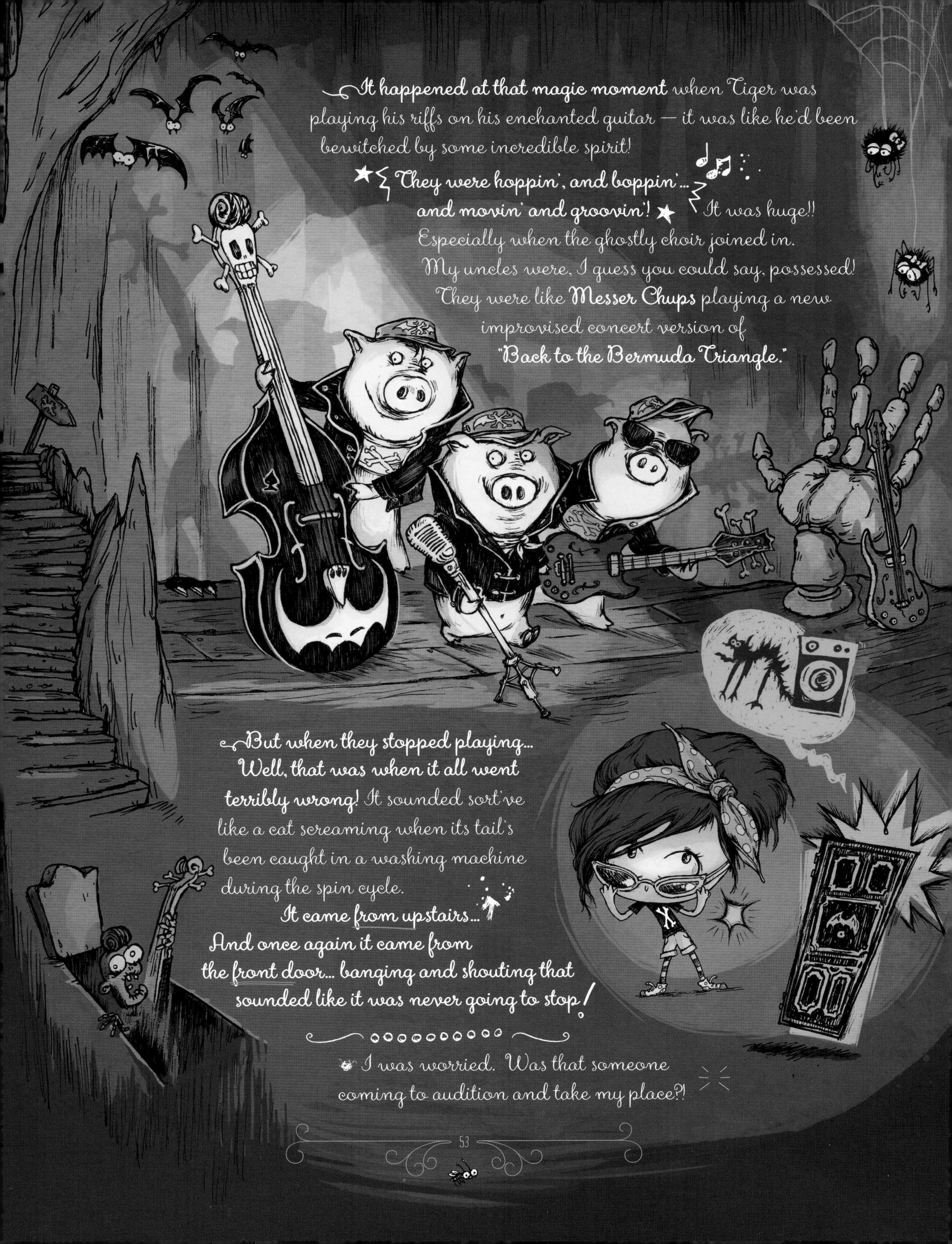

It happened at that magic moment when Tiger was playing his riffs on his enchanted guitar — it was like he'd been bewitched by some incredible spirit!

★ They were hoppin', and boppin'... and movin' and groovin'! ★ It was huge!! Especially when the ghostly choir joined in. My uncles were, I guess you could say, possessed! They were like **Messer Chups** playing a new improvised concert version of "Back to the Bermuda Triangle."

But when they stopped playing... Well, that was when it all went terribly wrong! It sounded sort've like a cat screaming when its tail's been caught in a washing machine during the spin cycle.

It came from upstairs...

And once again it came from the front door... banging and shouting that sounded like it was never going to stop!

I was worried. Was that someone coming to audition and take my place?!

HORROR PIE !!

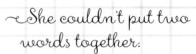

... When I finally got to the door, I discovered who our primal screamer was. Miss Grekinn, our _favorite_ neighbor!

She was holding out a steaming pie with three snow-white tibias sticking out! The "gift" had a silky scarlet (gulp!) ribbon around it.

She couldn't put two words together:

"...they... a... te... raw... cooked... everywhere, my Chester, everywhere... can't find... you've? Raw... co-cooked?"

Pretty certain that everything was okay, I told her not to worry — that it was just a mean trick. Someone was just mocking our traditional Sunday lunch horror pie... but, by the end of the morning, all the neighborhood grannies had come by, each having had their own delivery of pie!

Every one of them had the same dreadful (but delicious!) discovery at their front door. And after the jam jars and the flowers, they came to us... they couldn't take it anymore.

-"It sat there, quietly, addressed to me." \\ Snif! //
-"Look, there's even a little note so we know who to thank!" \\ Snif, snif! //

(Hankies, ladies, don't you think?)

Miss Grekinn
Our favorite neighbor

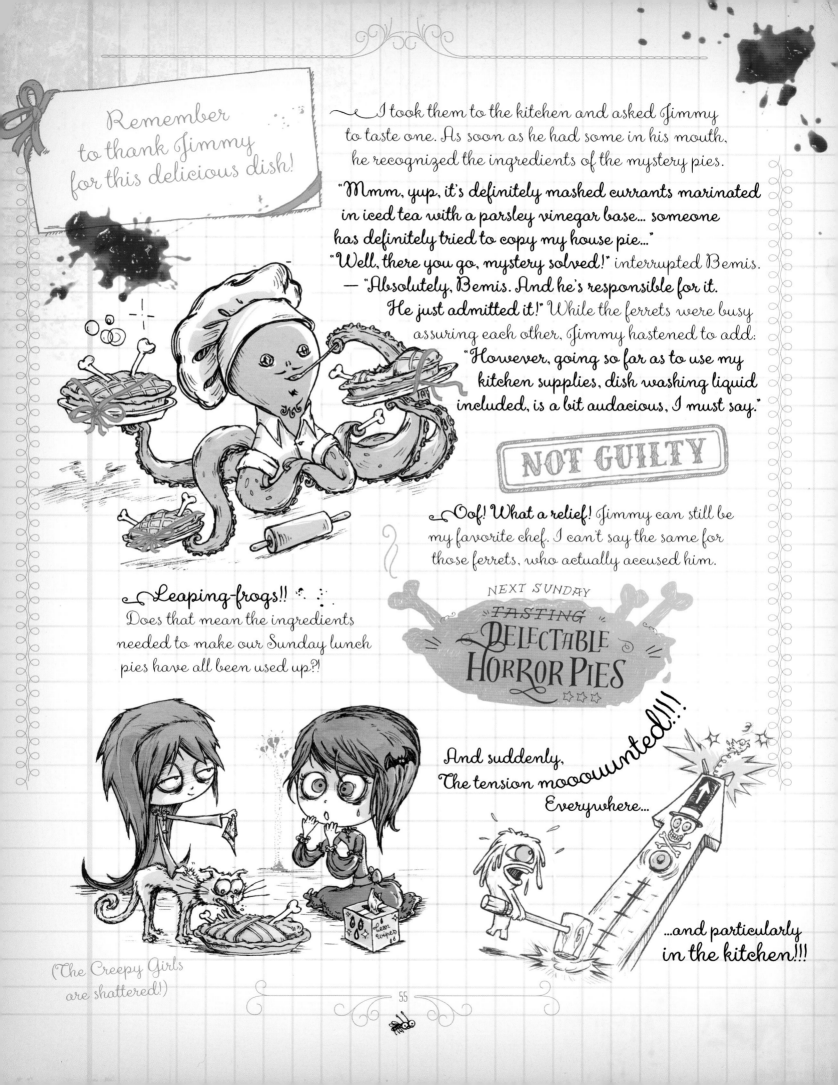

Remember to thank Jimmy for this delicious dish!

—I took them to the kitchen and asked Jimmy to taste one. As soon as he had some in his mouth, he recognized the ingredients of the mystery pies.

"Mmm, yup, it's definitely mashed currants marinated in iced tea with a parsley vinegar base... someone has definitely tried to copy my house pie..."

"Well, there you go, mystery solved!" interrupted Bemis.

— "Absolutely, Bemis. And he's responsible for it. He just admitted it!" While the ferrets were busy assuring each other, Jimmy hastened to add: "However, going so far as to use my kitchen supplies, dish washing liquid included, is a bit audacious, I must say."

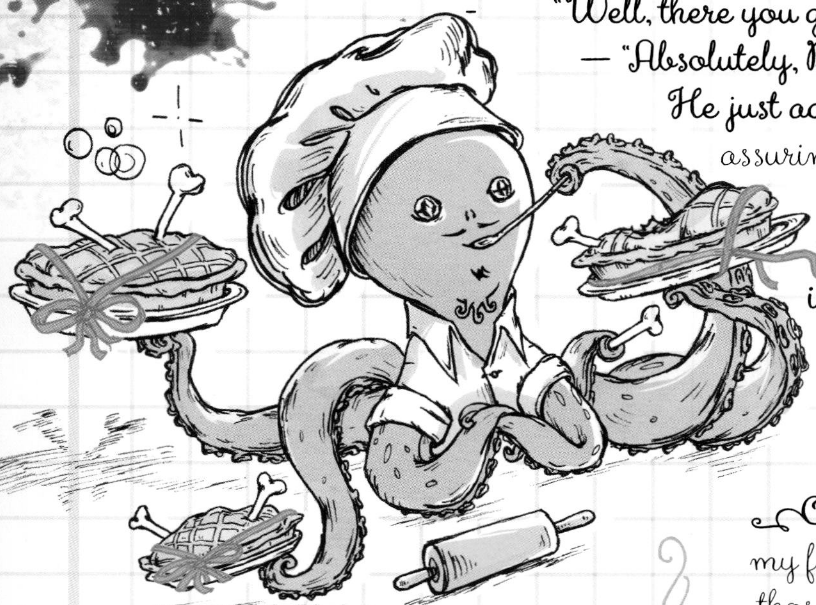

NOT GUILTY

Oof! What a relief! Jimmy can still be my favorite chef. I can't say the same for those ferrets, who actually accused him.

Leaping-frogs!! Does that mean the ingredients needed to make our Sunday lunch pies have all been used up?!

NEXT SUNDAY

~~TASTING~~

DELECTABLE HORROR PIES

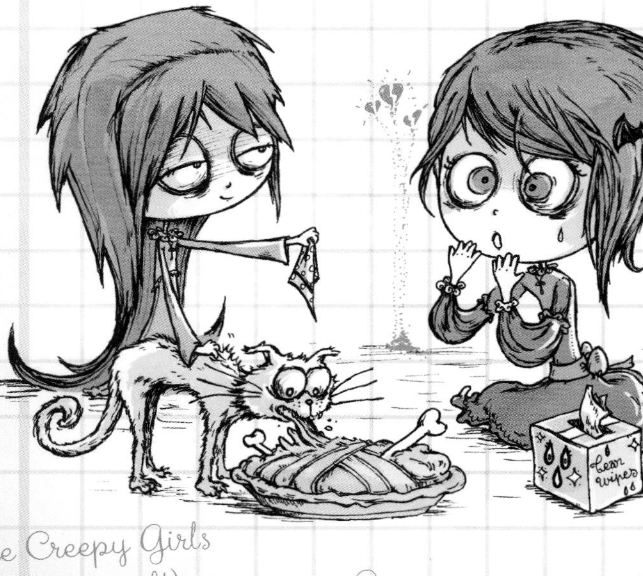

tear wipes

(The Creepy Girls are shattered!)

And suddenly, The tension mooouunted!!! Everywhere...

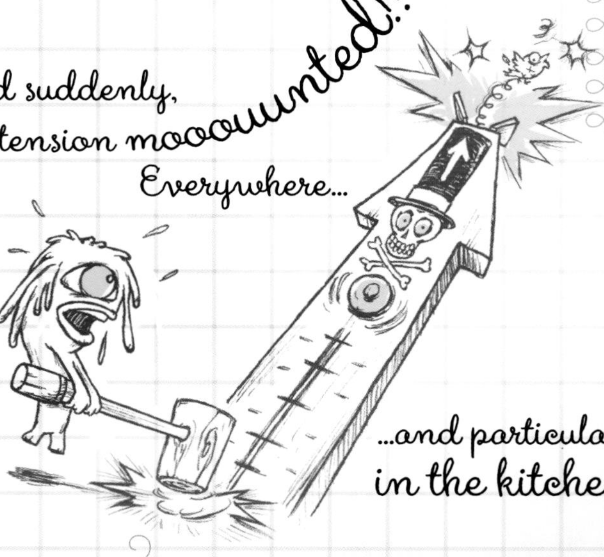

...and particularly in the kitchen!!!

Old FRIENDS Reunions AND RECONNAISSANCE

Unlike the other kitchen incidents, this time the guests were not the least bit amused by the disappearance of our special ingredients. It takes a lot to get them riled.

But, famous for their monstrous appetites... a meal-less mealtime could really wreak havoc.

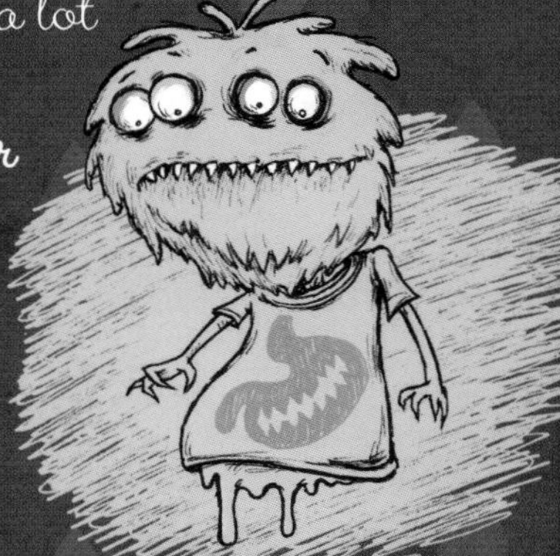

Something has to be done! And fast!! Especially since the rumor is spreading that our two furry detectives now **suspect my smaller uncle, Tiger Pig!!** According to them, he's been away a bit too often, claiming to be rehearsing his solos and... unfortunately for him (I have to say...) he is just the right height for the handprints found throughout the inn... **three apples high!**

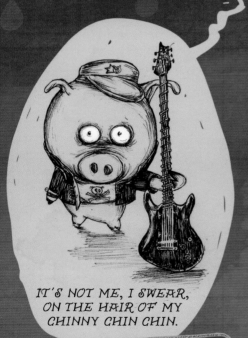

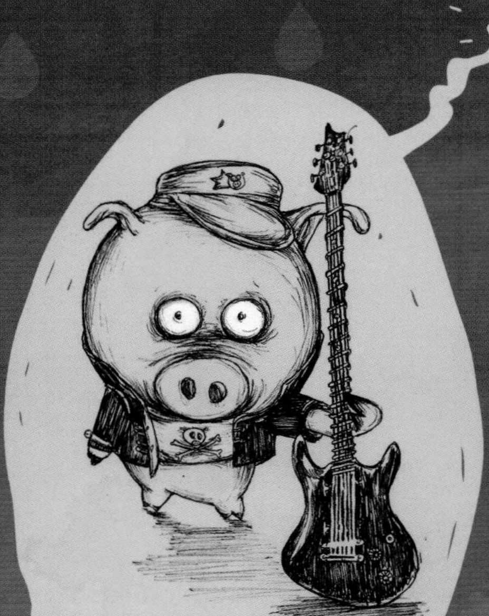
IT'S NOT ME, I SWEAR, ON THE HAIR OF MY CHINNY CHIN CHIN.

NOT GUILTY

Wanting to know the identity of our mysterious perpetrator, my uncles called an expert, actually a "profiler*," to get a better idea of what's going on. Fortunately, my uncles had installed a secret phone line for exactly this sort of thing. It was out of the question that one of them should stand accused of anything!!

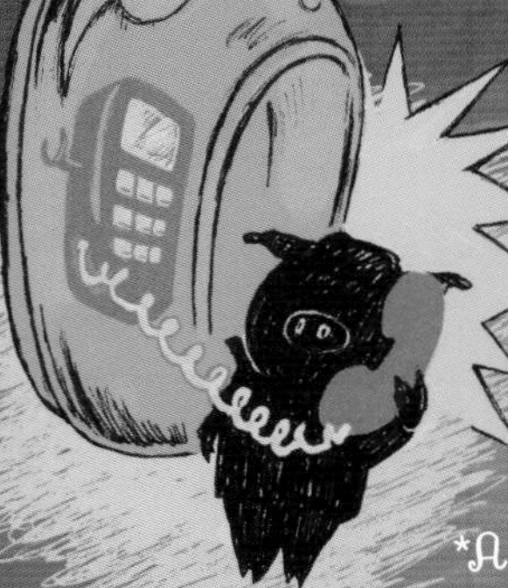

*A very clever investigator! Able to determine everything about someone in a flash!

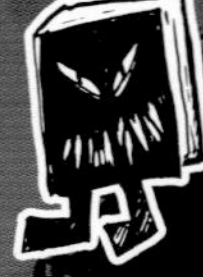

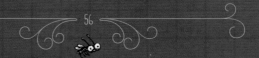

"UH YUP, WORD TRAVELS FAST! FOLKS ARE ALREADY SAYING THAT THE GRAY'S INN INN IS GOING TO BE A BIT LESS BUSY..."

Isn't it funny how often times when there's a problem we don't immediately see the quite obvious solution?

And especially considering that he came right over as soon as Stan (the coolest of my uncles) called him...

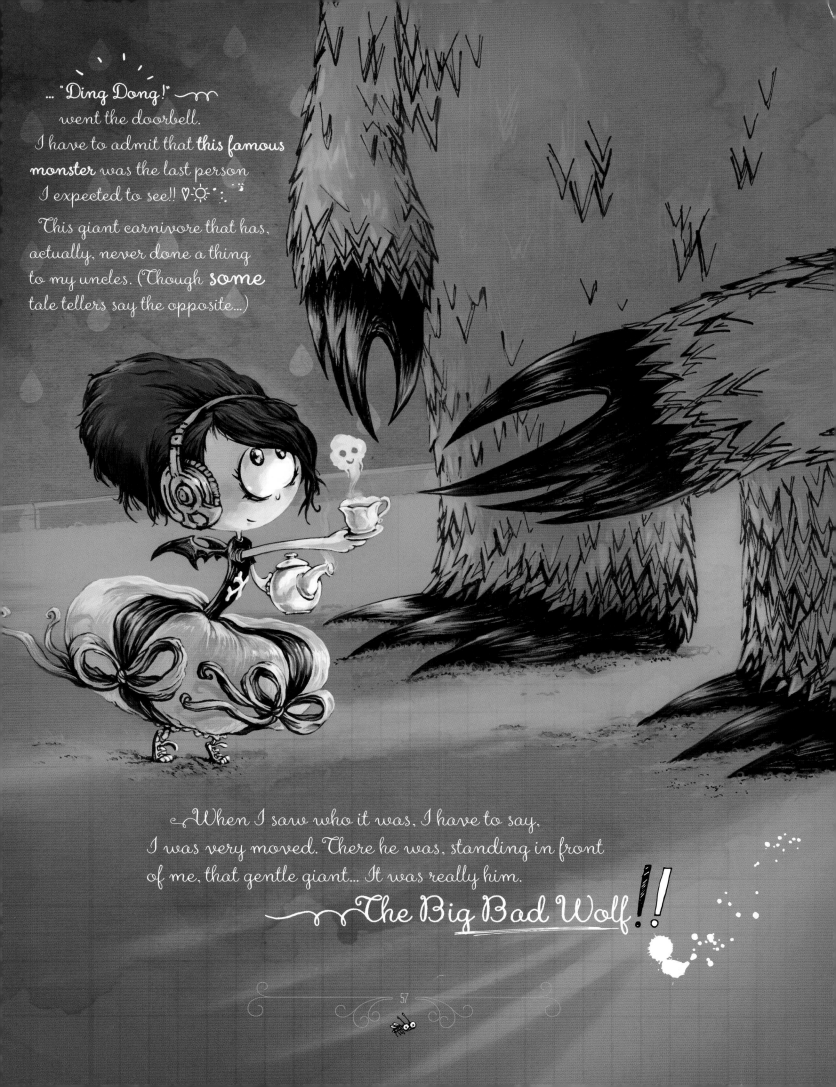

... "**Ding Dong!**"
went the doorbell.
I have to admit that **this famous monster** was the last person I expected to see!!

This giant carnivore that has, actually, never done a thing to my uncles. (Though **some** tale tellers say the opposite...)

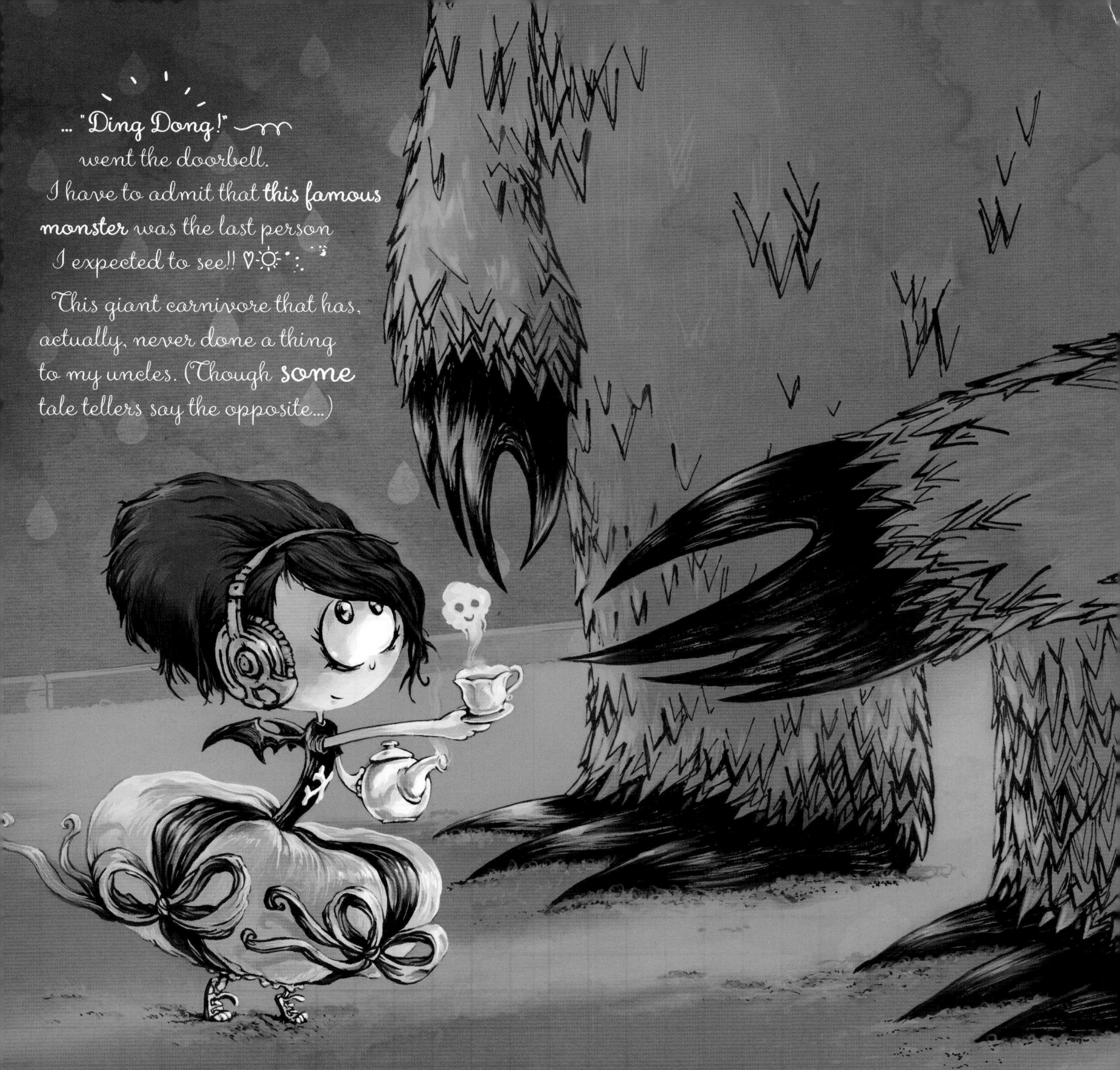

When I saw who it was, I have to say, I was very moved. There he was, standing in front of me, that gentle giant... It was really him.

The Big Bad Wolf!!

The BIG mystery NEARLY SOLVED

When he stepped into our little salon, it was like the cold North Wind had blown an icy gust straight into our bones. Had we all been somewhere deep in the Black Wood, we could not have felt more chilled.

The witches reached for their brooms, Amelia dove behind the sofa, and Smoug the Grey started smoking furiously... Only Little Red Riding Hood seemed to be unmoved.

Meanwhile, my uncles and the Wolf greeted each other and caught up.

- "Hello, Wolf, how ya been since we last saw ya?"

- "Good, I guess, same old, same old. Hasn't been much to huff and puff about since you guys moved away...

...I'm so glad you called, I was starting to get bored."

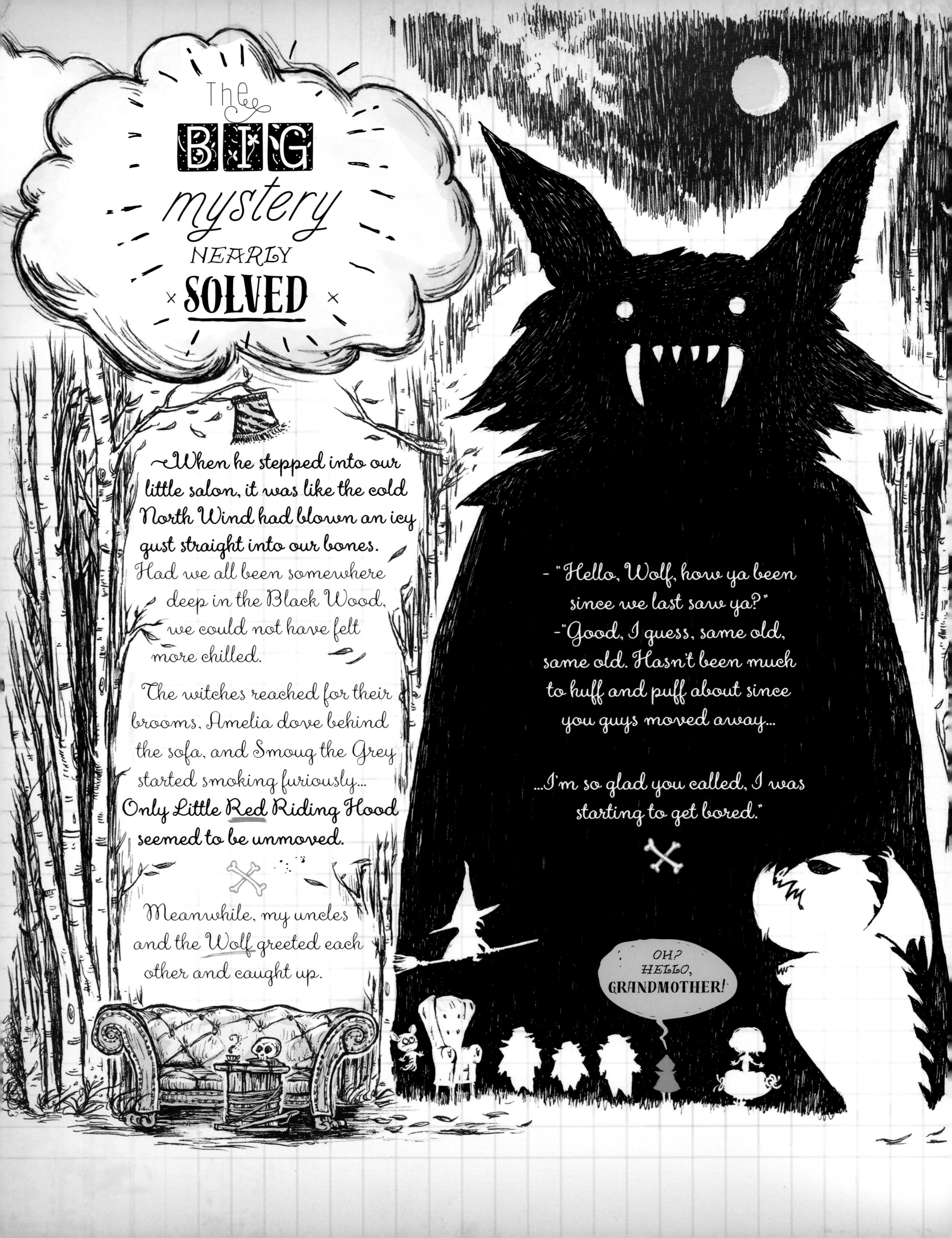
OH? HELLO, GRANDMOTHER!

The niceties over with and the cold air warmed, everyone was surprised by Miss Red's comment. She seemed to be a bit confused... **and was acting reeeealy strange!!**

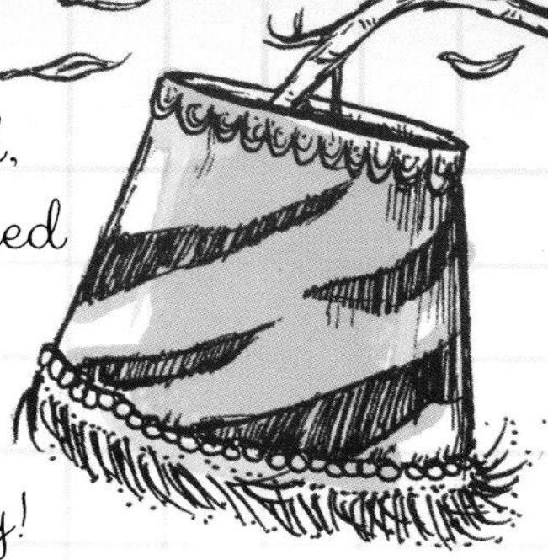

Confusing one of my favorite celebrities for a granny! To be honest, it really annoyed me...

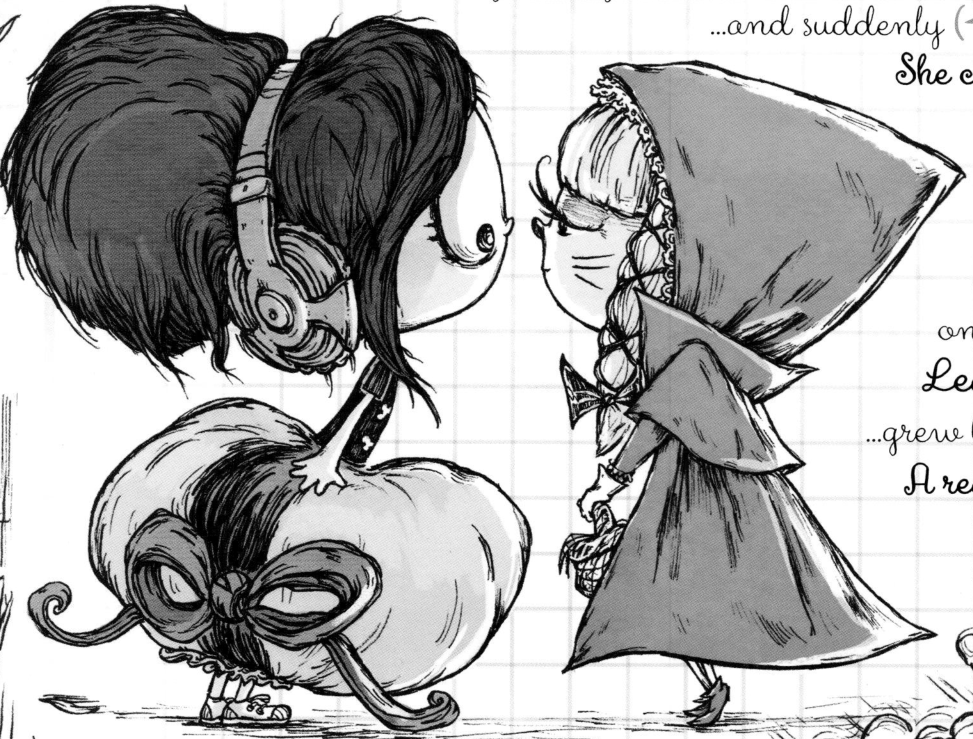

...and suddenly (Higgedy...)
She changed... (Piggedy!)
She grew facial hair!
There was a little
moustache under her
cute little nose and fuzz
on her face. And her eyes ...
Leaping-frogs!! (Oops!!)
...grew big and bright! (double oops!!)
A real little wolf, with braids!!

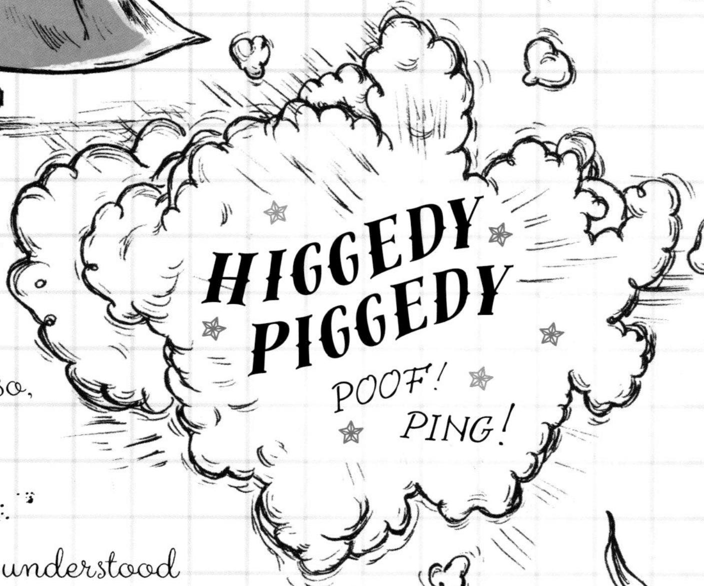
HIGGEDY PIGGEDY
POOF!
PING!

...and then... (Poof! Ping!) **the next second, she was herself again...** (or the self she was earlier anyway!)
...So little, so cute, and so tired, so much so, that she said she needed to take a nap!

And... zap! She was gone again!

I don't think anyone in the room really understood what I had done, except Wolf, who shot me a look in secret, before explaining to us that **Little Red Riding Hood was portal lagged from her trip from Fairytale Land...**

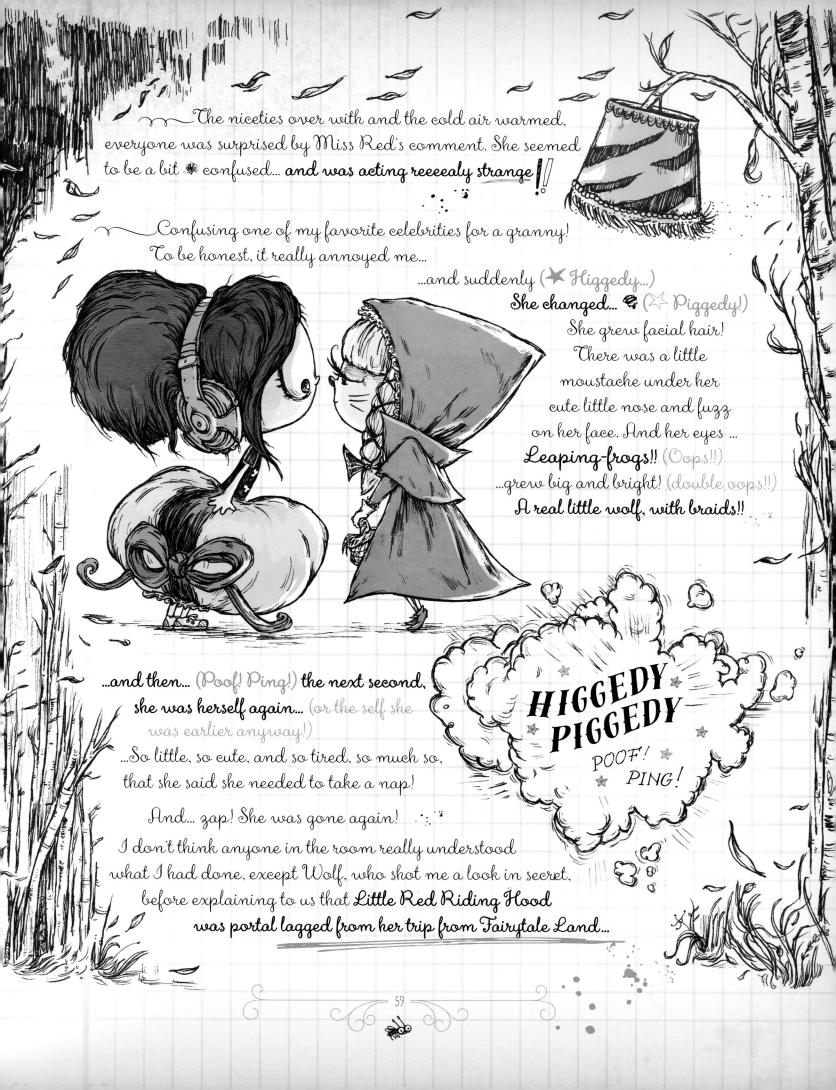

EXCELLENT a SICK Machiavellian PLAN

Big Bad Wolf has made it clear,
That things are not as they appear,
The cat is finally out of the bag,
Red Riding Hood's suffering from portal lag!

And he went on to explain:

"The way I see it, there is no mystery at all. Miss Red is discombobulated from her tiring trip from Fairytale Land. London has her a little scared! She can't find her grandmother, so she is finding comfort in **trying to recreate her fairytale, but she can't get it right!** And that's what got her talking to herself and causing jam, flower and pie problems. But her recent little transformation, that's something else entirely..."

(He glanced at me and said: ... "...which is none of my business, really.")

(Phew!)

In order for it to stop, we needed to catch her! (Oops!) But, (believe you me) catching someone from Fairytale Land who wants to stay free, is simply not easy. **So in order to avoid some sort of long, dragged out Hollywood-style chase scene, one of my uncles came up with a great plan:**

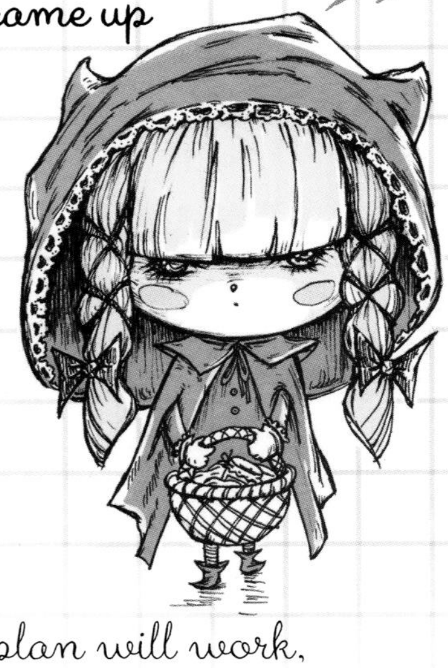

☆ Get her attention!

Lure her with a present of the best **scary pastries.**

☆ The Plan!

To be sure that the plan will work, we have to be discreet. That's why he suggested we trick her with a forgery: **A fake letter from her grandmother.**

My dearest,

I am at the inn. I brought you a present full of sweet surprises. It's downstairs in the dining room. Be a dear and bring it to me. It was too heavy for me to carry, though I am sure it will be no trouble for you. You are so nice and so wonderful and I love you so much.

I can't wait to see you again.

Your loving Grandmother.

(I'm in room 15.)

Tiger's idea — he's the smartest one!

(This fake was composed and written by my youngest uncle — an expert forger and master cheater..... It's not very honest, that's true, but what do you expect from a guy who is so small everyone thinks he's a piglet?!)

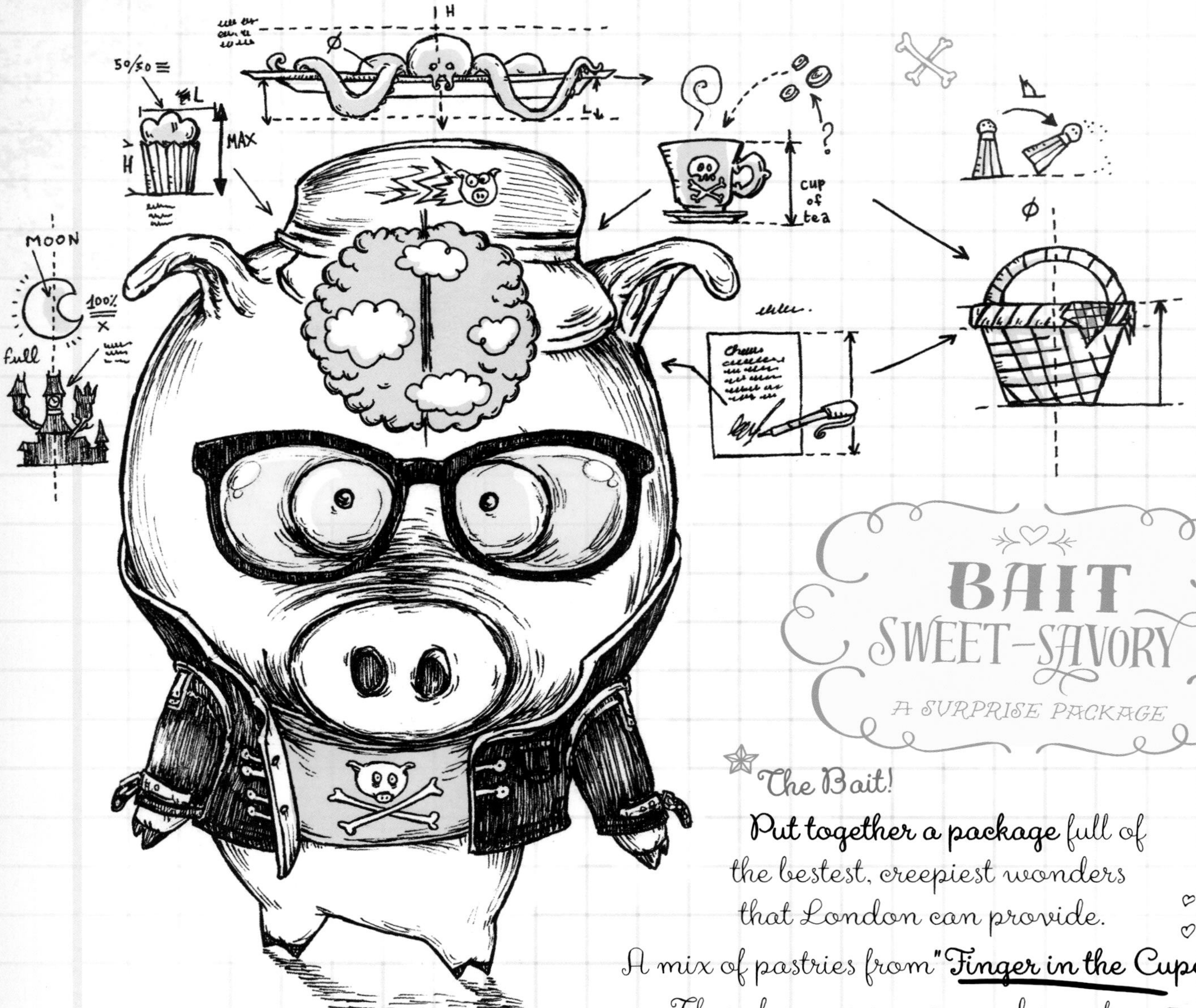

50/50
MAX
MOON
100%
full
cup of tea

BAIT
SWEET-SAVORY
A SURPRISE PACKAGE

The Bait!

Put together a package full of the bestest, creepiest wonders that London can provide.

A mix of pastries from "**Finger in the Cupcake**"!

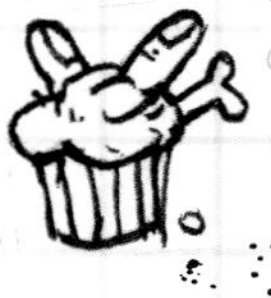

These famous savory and sweet baked goods have fingers in the icing. They are perfect for monsters dying for a crunchy little snack.

The trap!

It's foolproof because the gift is from her grandmother and since **that's who she's obsessed with, nothing can go wrong.**

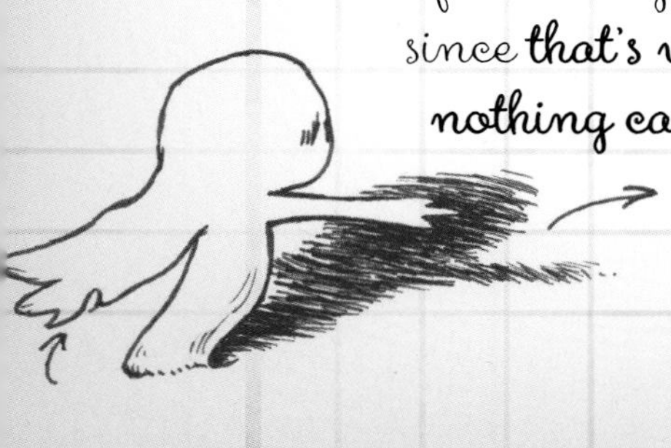

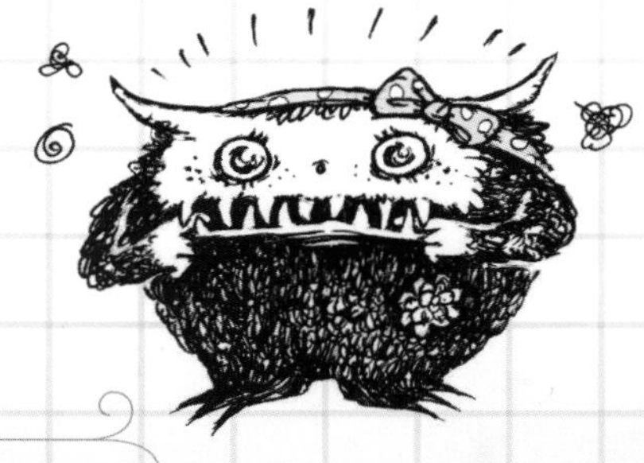

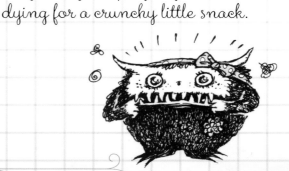

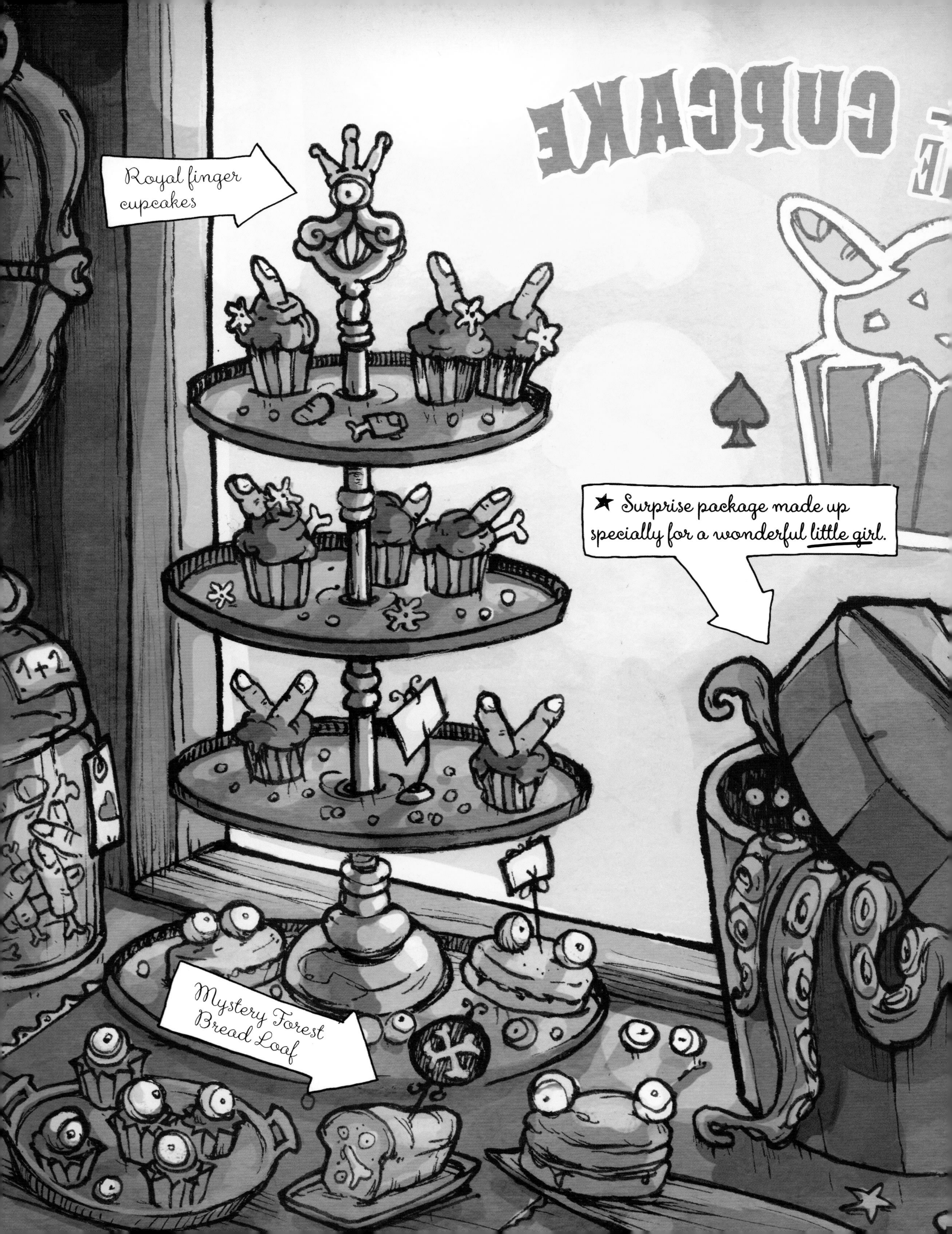
CUPCAKE
Royal finger cupcakes
★ Surprise package made up specially for a wonderful little girl.
1+2
Mystery Forest Bread Loaf

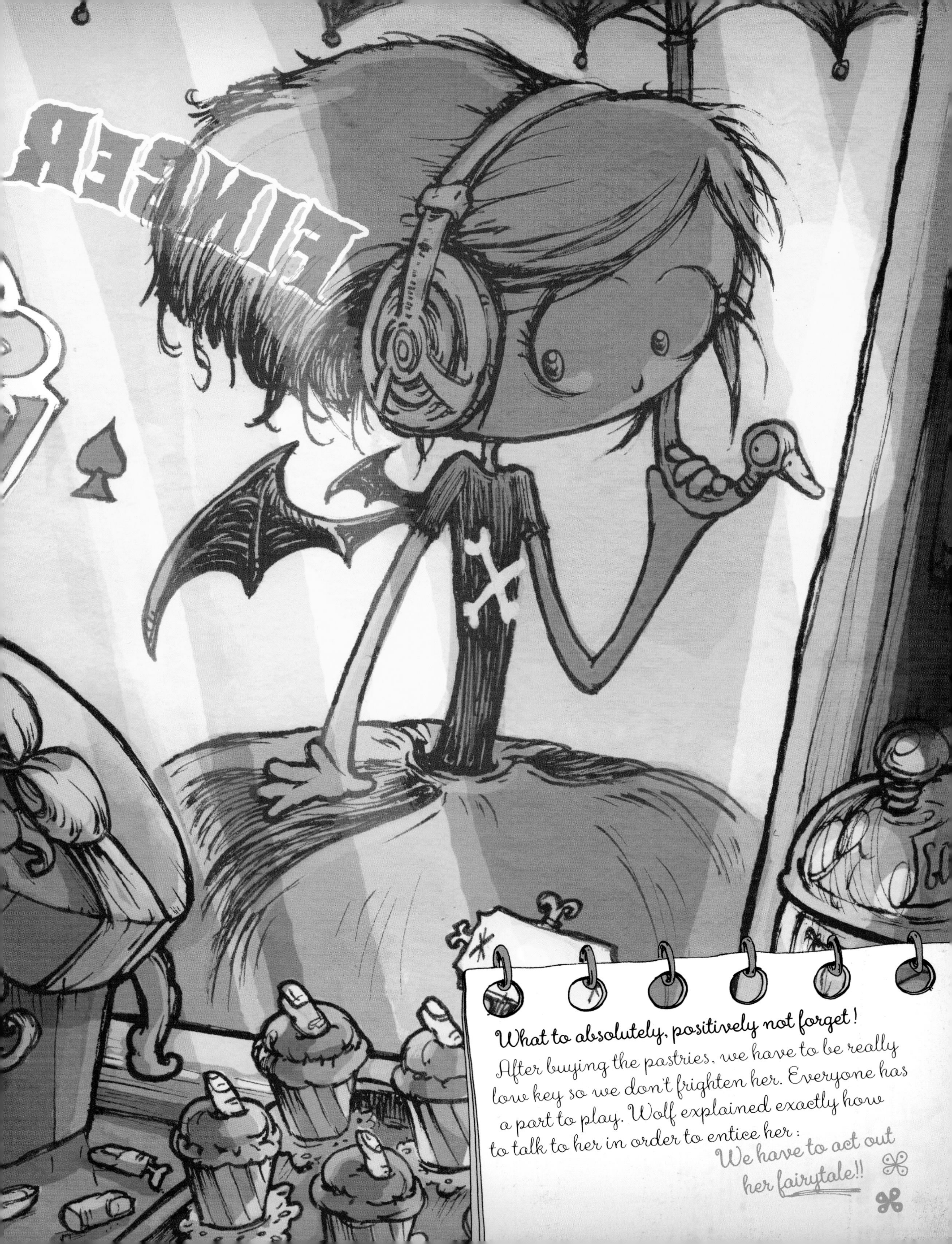

What to absolutely, positively not forget!

After buying the pastries, we have to be really low key so we don't frighten her. Everyone has a part to play. Wolf explained exactly how to talk to her in order to entice her:

We have to act out her fairytale!!

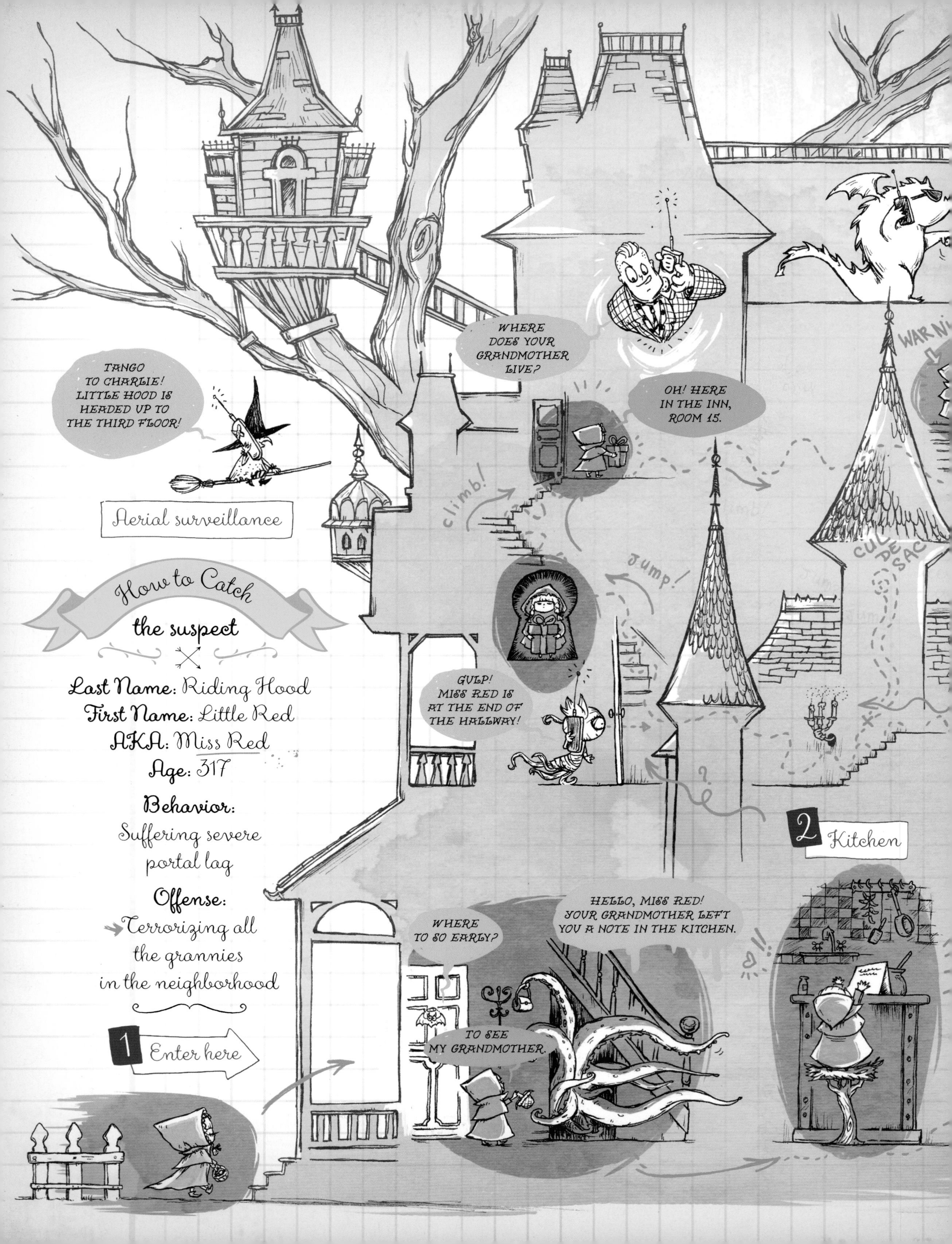
TANGO TO CHARLIE! LITTLE HOOD IS HEADED UP TO THE THIRD FLOOR!
Aerial surveillance
WHERE DOES YOUR GRANDMOTHER LIVE?
OH! HERE IN THE INN, ROOM 15.
climb!
jump!
CUL DE SAC
GULP! MISS RED IS AT THE END OF THE HALLWAY!
How to Catch the suspect
Last Name: Riding Hood
First Name: Little Red
AKA: Miss Red
Age: 317
Behavior:
Suffering severe portal lag
Offense:
Terrorizing all the grannies in the neighborhood
1 Enter here
2 Kitchen
WHERE TO SO EARLY?
HELLO, MISS RED! YOUR GRANDMOTHER LEFT YOU A NOTE IN THE KITCHEN.
TO SEE MY GRANDMOTHER.

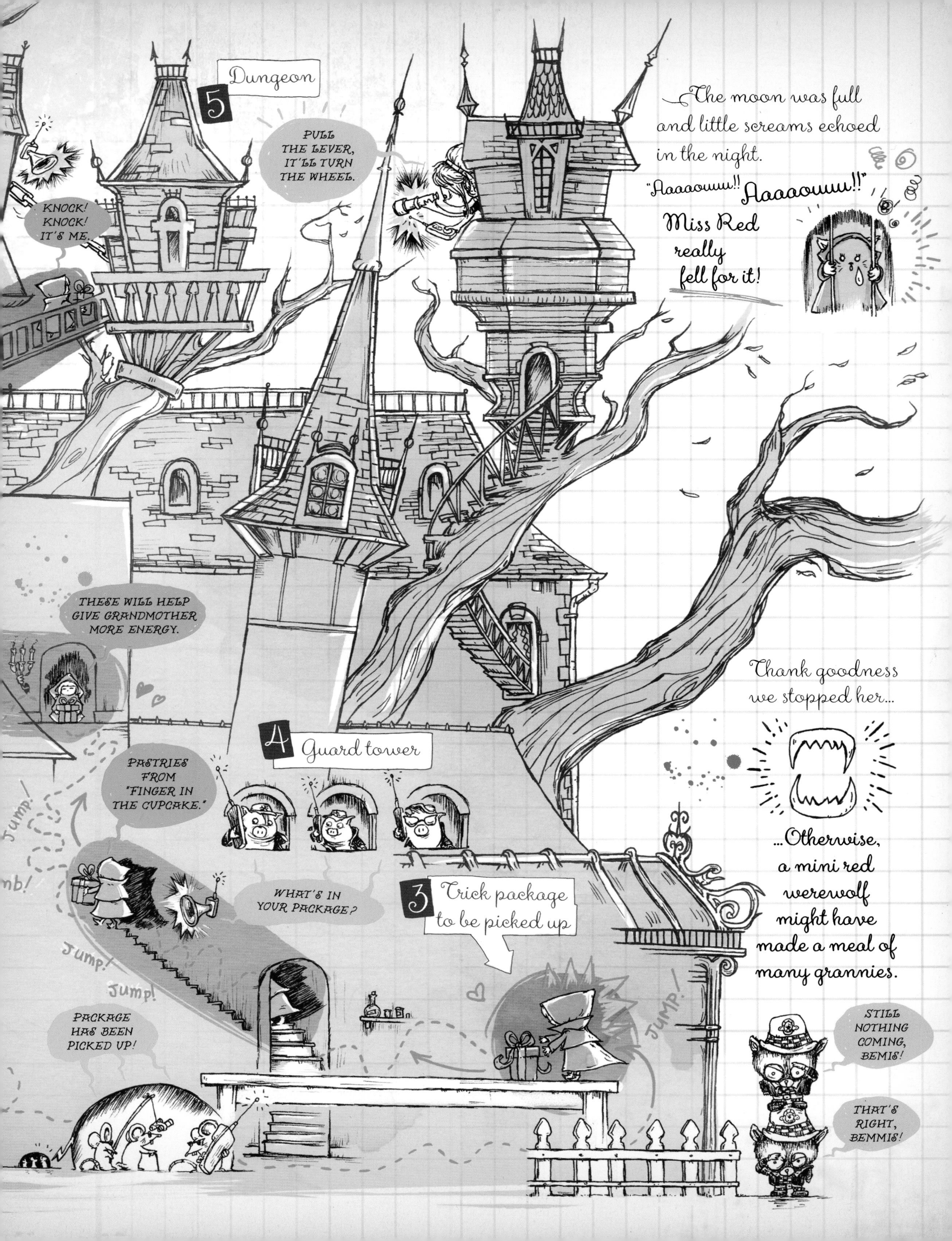

5 Dungeon
KNOCK! KNOCK! IT'S ME.
PULL THE LEVER, IT'LL TURN THE WHEEL.
The moon was full and little screams echoed in the night.
"Aaaaouuu!! Aaaaouuu!!"
Miss Red really fell for it!
THESE WILL HELP GIVE GRANDMOTHER MORE ENERGY.
4 Guard tower
PASTRIES FROM "FINGER IN THE CUPCAKE."
Jump!
WHAT'S IN YOUR PACKAGE?
3 Trick package to be picked up
Jump!
Jump!
JUMP!
PACKAGE HAS BEEN PICKED UP!
Thank goodness we stopped her...
...Otherwise, a mini red werewolf might have made a meal of many grannies.
STILL NOTHING COMING, BEMIS!
THAT'S RIGHT, BEMMIS!

When we went upstairs to get her, she was sleeping like a baby. It was like a real-life fairytale...

But we were pretty shocked to see **she had transformed into an adorable little Hooded Wolf!!**

(Which was probably going to upset her grandmother!)

And then...

HIGGEDY PIGGEDY

POOF! PING!

...The magic spell broke and she was back to her original self, **the authentic cute Little Red Riding Hood.** My uncles gave me a rather severe look. I guess they'd realized I'd played a big part in what, from then on, would be known as

a Strange Tale. ★

(Oops and double oops!)

Once upon a time, in the heart of London, there were three little pigs that had a very strange niece.

Her skin was as white as milk and her hair was as black as silk...

When she was born, her godmother gave her a special gift, the ability to change anything that bored her. So, when Little Red Riding Hood turned into a little wolf, who do you think was to blame?...

...Spooky of course!

...Who got bored when her nose got a tickle from the hairs of a cat who was licking off jam from a jar left on the mat, her sneeze blew his hair up like a back-comb and shampoo. Luckily Ms. Grekinn thought it was long overdue!

...Who got bored when having to handle a frustrated ghost instead of being in class with her favorite chef host!

...and overly bored when her favorite celebrity star was mocked and called grandma by some Miss, quite bizarre!!

Yes, Miss Red was confused, but come on, do you really think Spooky's little prank would make that Little Red wolverine start munching on grannies!!!

"MORAL: IT'S BEST NOT TO BORE A LITTLE GIRL WHO HAS A SPECIAL POWER FROM HER FAIRY GODMOTHER!"

— Epilogue —

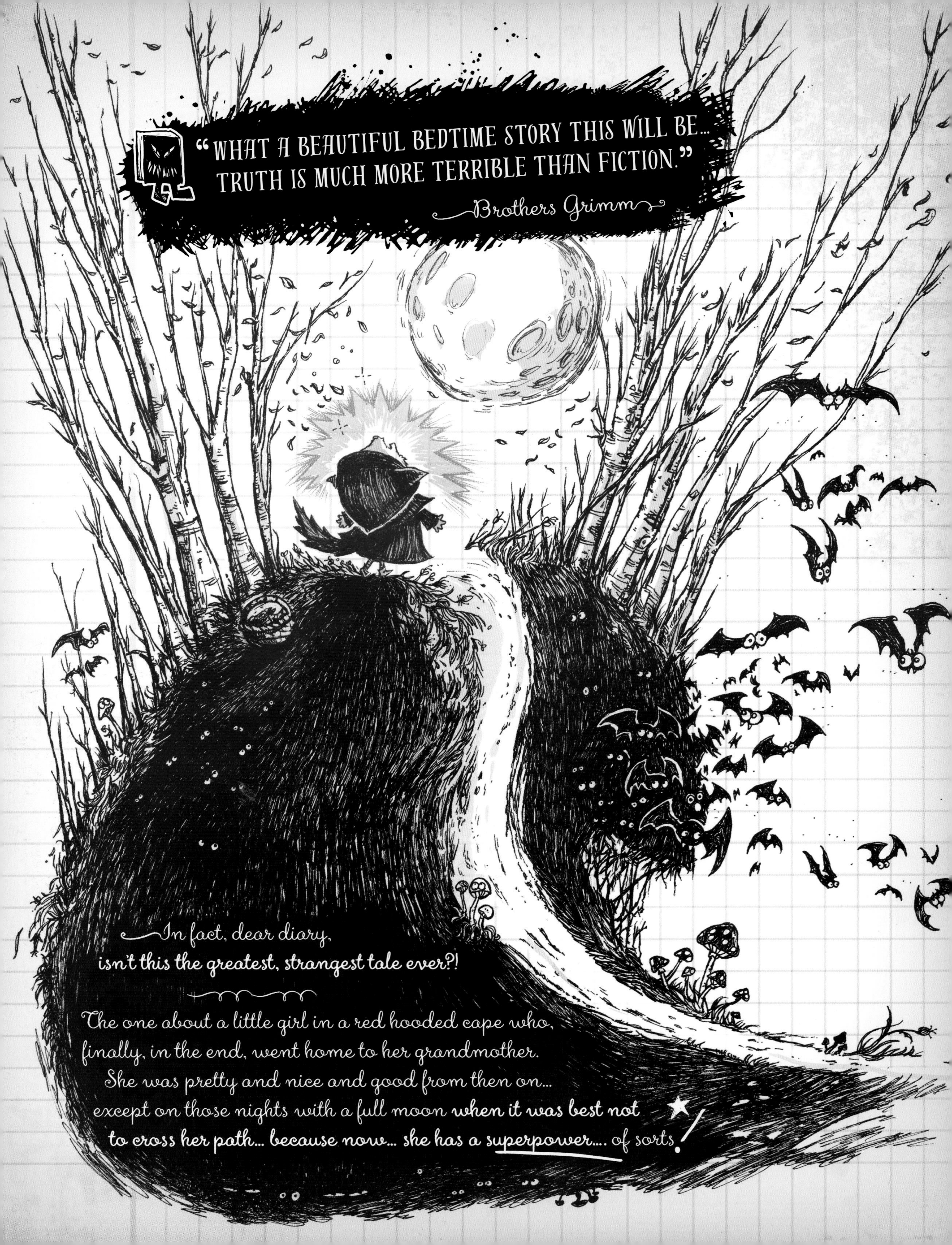

"WHAT A BEAUTIFUL BEDTIME STORY THIS WILL BE...
TRUTH IS MUCH MORE TERRIBLE THAN FICTION."

— Brothers Grimm

—In fact, dear diary,
isn't this the greatest, strangest tale ever?!

The one about a little girl in a red hooded cape who,
finally, in the end, went home to her grandmother.
She was pretty and nice and good from then on...
except on those nights with a full moon when it was best not
to cross her path... because now... she has a superpower.... of sorts!

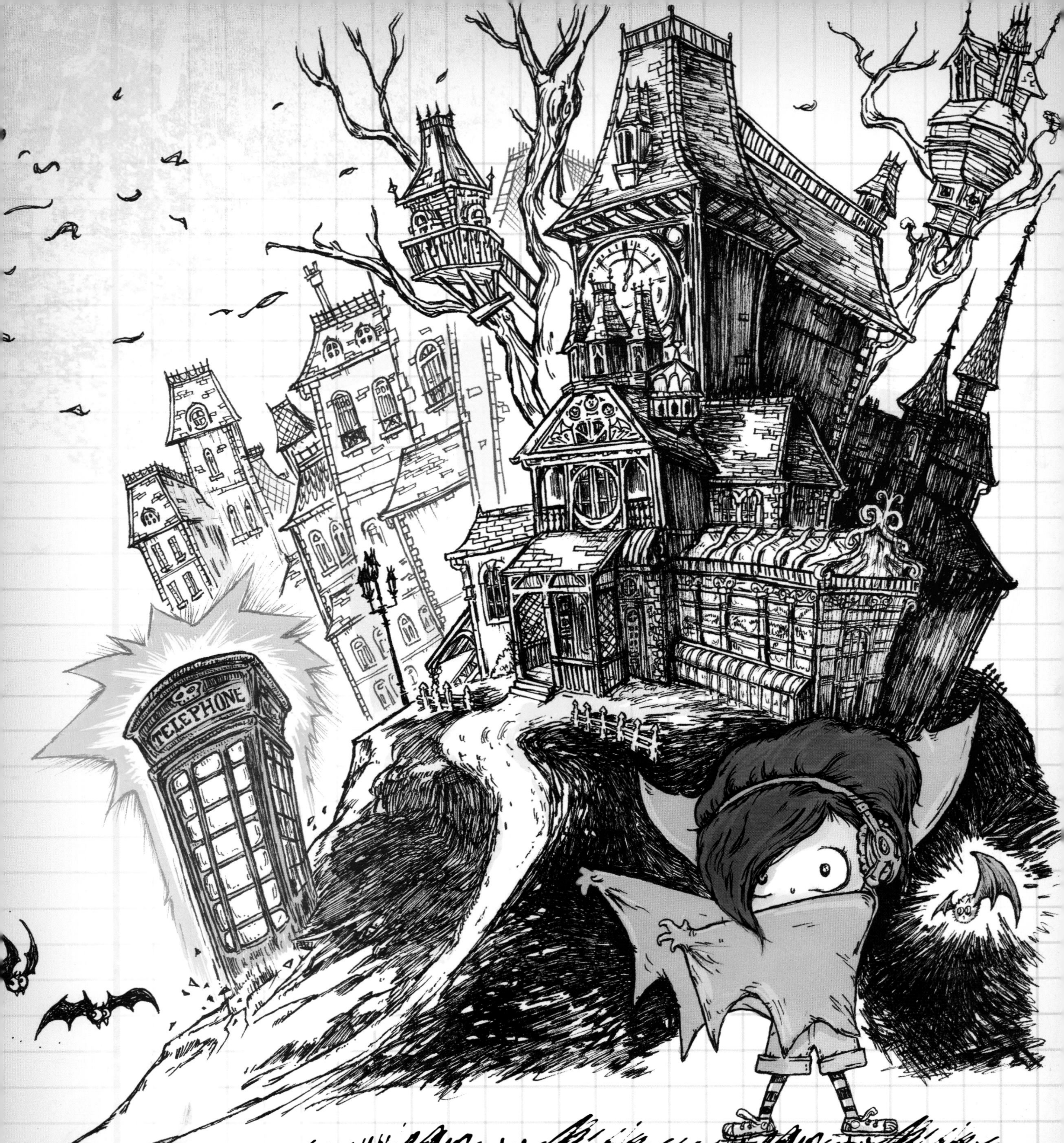
TELEPHONE

"A BIT LIKE THIS LITTLE GIRL: 'BETTER NOT STAY OUT TOO LATE
CAUSE YOU MIGHT END UP AS PART OF SPOOKY'S FATE!'
HA! HA! HA! HA!... HAAA!"

(but that's a whole other story...)

Books I RECOMMEND

~ Carine-M and Élian Black'mor have done a ton of cool projects together... *(I know you'll love 'em)*

All the illustrations and stories (except the one about the phantom) are by them.

★ Collections:

Black'Mor Chronicles — the tales of a dragon hunter:

– *In Search of Lost Dragons* (Dynamite Entertainment)
Sur la Piste des Dragon Oubliés (Editons Glénat)
The journals of Elian Black'mor, the famous traveler and global surveyor
who is on a 'round the world journey on a mission to find and make a record
of those legendary creatures: Dragons.

– *The Cursed, Welcome to the Park of the Chimeras* (Insight Editions)
Les Maudits, Bienvenue au Parc des Chimères (Editions Glénat)
In Victorian London's parks, fog obscures portals where myth and reality merge ...
The most prevalent one is the Park of the Chimeras: a deeply magical place where
the children of Pan, Lycans, Hydras and other Titans can find refuge ...

More Spooky & the Strange Tales;

– *Spooky & les contes de Travers – Tome 2 - Charmant Vampire* (Editons Glénat)
Spooky & the Strange Tales - volume 2 – A Charming Vampire
(not yet available in English, stand by...)
Everyone loves a love story! And charming princes and their lovely (frogs') legs...
Well, me too! And especially with a spicy sauce!

– *Spooky & les contes de Travers – Tome 3 - Princess Creepy* (Editons Glénat)
Spooky & the Strange Tales - volume 3 – Creepy Princess
(not yet available in English, stand by...)

– *Guide du Savoir-Vivre en Compagnie des "Monstres"* (Kensington-Pudding)
How to Handle Monsters, A Monster Survival Guide.
(not yet available in English, stand by...)

Ghost Hunter ;

– *L'Effroyable encyclopedie des revenants* (Editons Glénat)
Encyclopedia of Ghosts (not yet available in English, stand by...)

– *L'Epouvantable encyclopedie des Fantomes* (Editons Glénat)
Terrifying Encyclopedia of Phantoms (not yet available in English, stand by...)

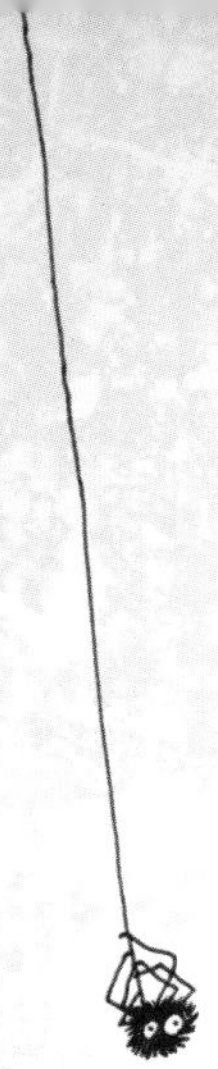

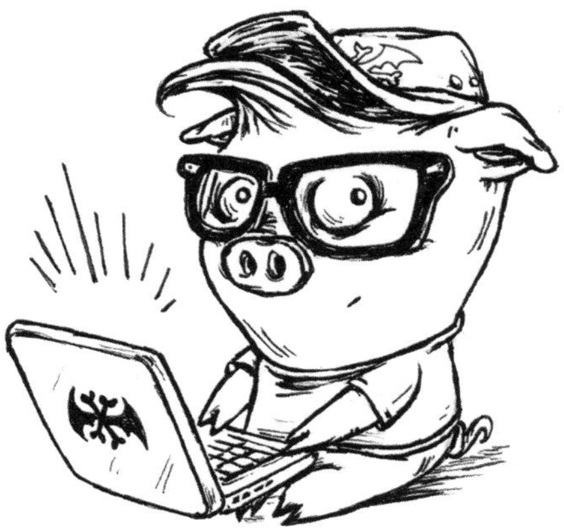

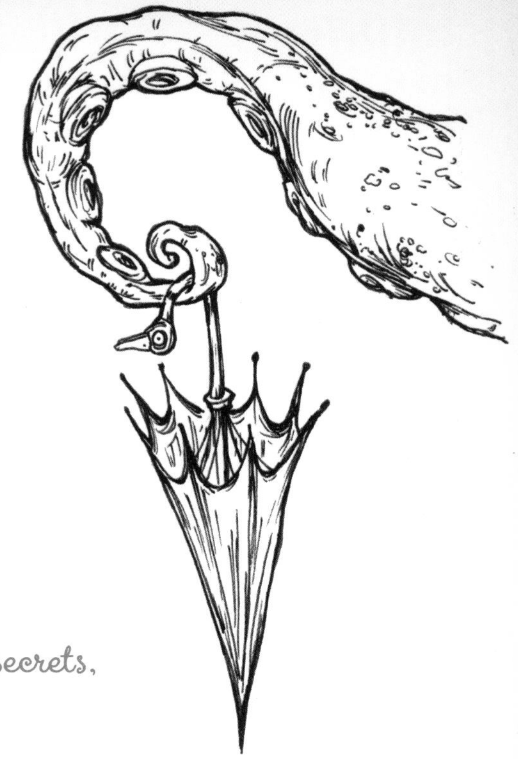

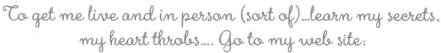

To get me live and in person (sort of)...learn my secrets, my heart throbs.... Go to my web site:

www.spooky-et-lescontesdetravers.com

To know more about the authors, enter their studio here:

www.arsenic-et-bouledegomme.com

To see even more of what they have done, go to their web sites:
www.carine-m.com – www.elian-black-mor.com

Edited by Justin Eisinger and Alonzo Simon
Publisher: Ted Adams

English translation and adaptation by:
Ivanka Hahnenberger & Donald Kersey

Lettered by:
Carine-m & Élian Black'mor

ISBN: 978-1-63140-934-9
20 19 18 17 1 2 3 4

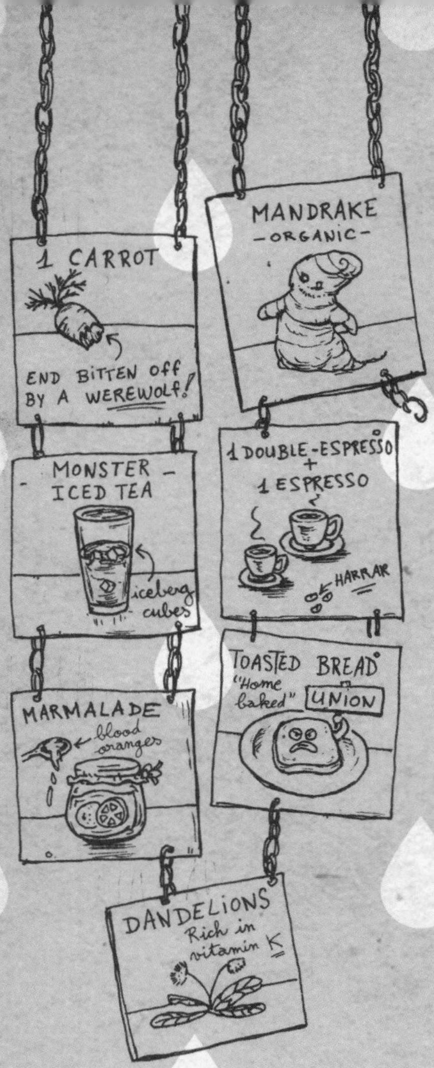
1 CARROT
END BITTEN OFF BY A WEREWOLF!
MANDRAKE
-ORGANIC-
MONSTER ICED TEA
iceberg cubes
1 DOUBLE-ESPRESSO + 1 ESPRESSO
HARRAR
MARMALADE
blood oranges
TOASTED BREAD
"Home baked"
UNION
DANDELIONS
Rich in vitamin K

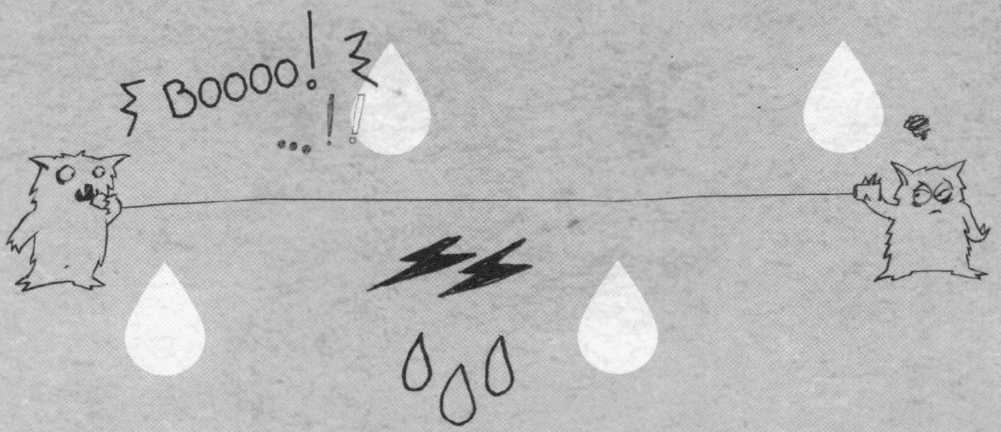
BOOOO!
...!!

× × × × × ×

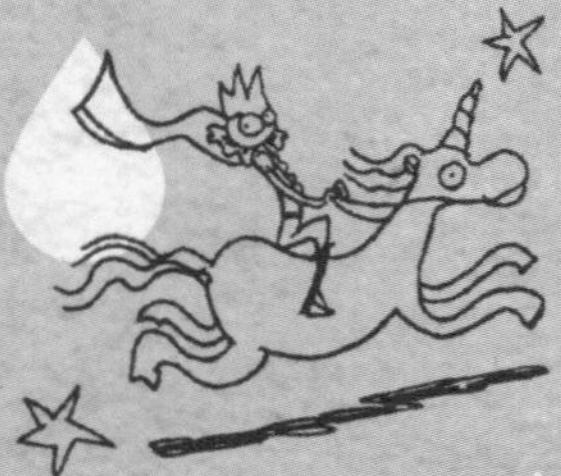

xoxo

To my monster for all eternity... C.

To my lovely little tinkerbell! E.

A huge thank you to Benoit C. the "creepiest" of editors!

And of course Ivanka, who gave life to this English version.

Spooky

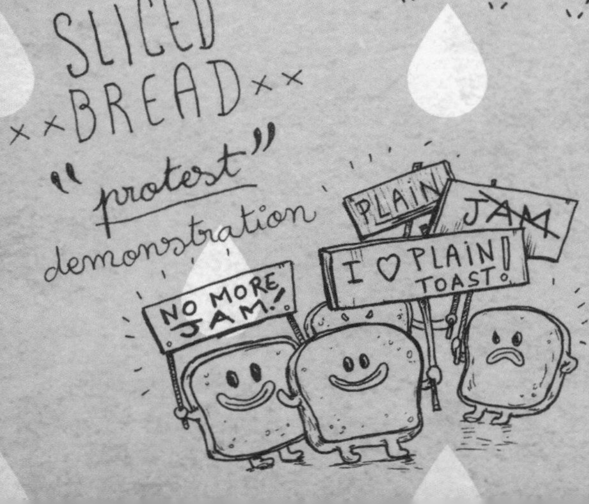
SLICED BREAD
"protest" demonstration
PLAIN
JAM
I ♥ PLAIN! TOAST
NO MORE JAM!

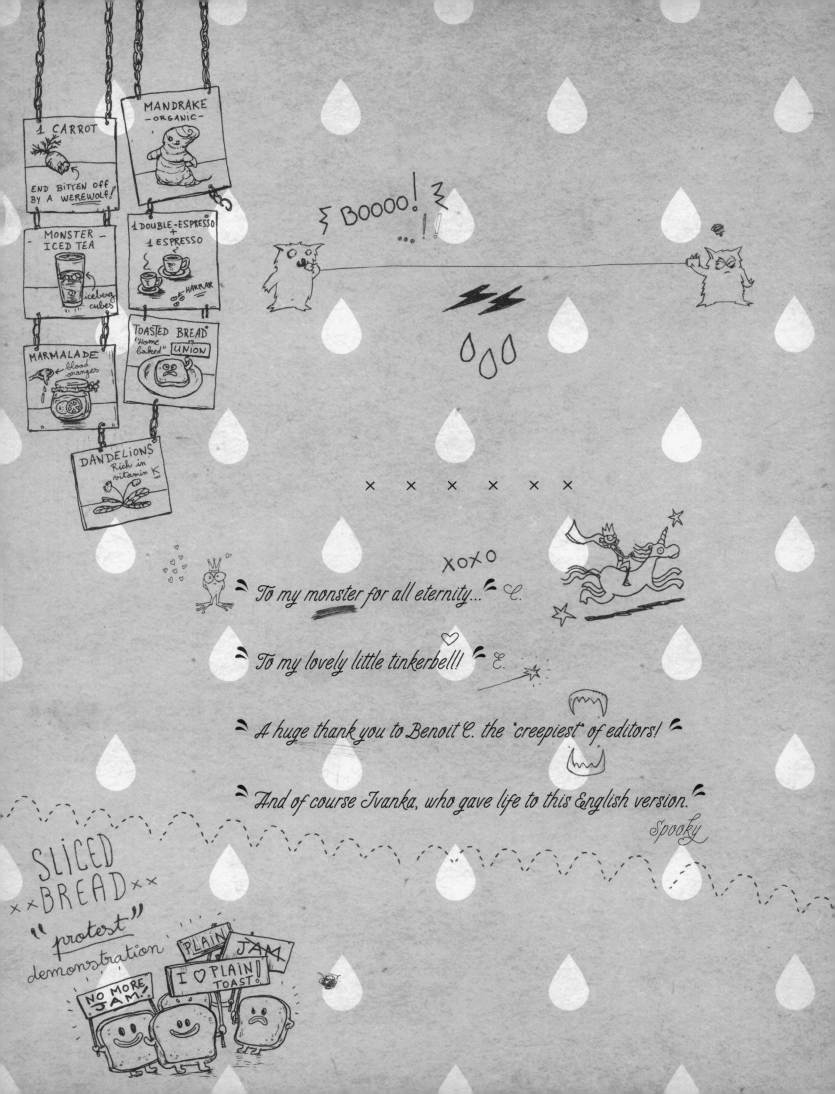